MW01017383

GIRL
IT'S NOT YOU

(it's definitely him)

CHRONICLES OF EPICALLY BAD DATES
from the
WOMEN WHO SURVIVED THEM

By Megan Edwards & Janet Reynolds
"THE UND8ABLES"

contents

13.

NICE GUYS ...
Or are they?!

49.

MEN WITH ISSUES ...
So many issues.

119.

BODILY FUNCTION MISHAPS

135.

RANDOM OCCURRENCES

169.

HAPPY ENDINGS
(No. not those ones.)

This little book with big heart is dedicated to all of you fiercely strong, powerful women—you are not alone in your quest for love! When you need to be reminded of that, reach for this book. It has superpowers. If that doesn't work, drink wine, put on a sexy outfit, and hit the town. It has always worked for us!

Oh, hi there!!! Welcome to our little book.

Let's start by introducing ourselves. We're Megan and Janet, and we're single-aholics.

Not too surprisingly, because we have both spent mucho time in the single department, we crossed paths—in an audition room for the show *First Dates Canada*, to be exact.

It was a hot May evening and Janet's friend, who'd come along for support, couldn't stand the stuffiness of the waiting room. It was a feeling Megan was all too familiar with after auditioning for the past 20 years (usually without success).

So Janet's friend left, and Janet took a seat beside Megan.

Megan: It was a decision she would later regret. Kidding!

It was a decision that would change the course of our lives drastically. Most of the pre-audition conversation focused on our battle with finding good men and our careers. I work in radio and television, and Janet is in the healthcare sector—complete opposites if you ask us! We then moved onto the topic of being epically single. We've each had a few long-term relationships and A LOT of hella bad dates.

Janet: We were excited about the fact that we could be on TV, but also because we could meet the man of our dreams. Little did we know that our lives were about to change—but only because of this chance meeting with each other.

(Megan is screaming "Girl Power!" as we type this).

Before we take you on an epic journey of all of our dating fails and those of friends far and wide, perhaps we should let you get to know us a little first.

Megan: Even as a 14-year-old, I knew I didn't want to be married in my 20s, but I thought I'd at least have a certain gentleman in mind by the time I turned 30.

As I turned 30 this past year—back in my hometown, with my old friends, single, drunk—I was about to hook up with an ex-boyfriend I hadn't seen for five years. Yeahhhh, a new low, even for me.

I've always been a strong, independent woman who wants to take care of herself. I've been adamant about making something of myself and making it on my own. I didn't realize that all my boyfriends would suffer along the way because of my unhappiness with my slow-growing career (realllyyyyyy, reallllyyyyy slow!) and the reality that they were never enough to fill that void for me.

My fucked-up-ed-ness aside, I've always thought the perfect person for me was out there, right around the next corner. Little did I know that there would be complete and utter fuckery along the way.

It's been quite the adventure and I knew I had to find a way to share it with all the single ladies, all the single ladies!

(Megan, you did NOT just bring Beyoncé into this!? That's next-level shit.)

Janet: I was always going to be the first of my friends to settle down, get married, pop out a couple of kids, and live happily ever after.

It's what I wanted and still want. I think. But I'm pretty sure my ovaries shrivel up a little more with each bad date and mediocre relationship I endure. There is a possibility that one (or let's face it, both) may roll out of the bottom of my pant leg when I cough one day.

I had my very first kiss at age 11, in a field by my house. Little did I know it was the start of men wreaking havoc on my life. As I've shared my dating shenanigans with friends (usually during some drunken night of debauchery where I end up crying or vomiting on myself), I've been told on numerous occasions to write a book.

"You gotta write this shit down!"

I always get the "How can you be single?" verbal backhand, or the "It'll happen when you least expect it" pity proverb. No matter who makes the comment, I want to throat punch them.

All kidding aside, how difficult can it be to find the guy I want to spend the rest of my life with? I know I'm not the only woman out there feeling this way. You, reading this, may feel that way also. Let's embark on a journey, and perhaps, after a few laughs (at us) and "ah ha" moments, we can answer this cosmic question together.

Stay tuned for our compilation of dates from absolute hell, online disasters, major creeps and just plain questionable behaviour. And in case you're trying to figure out who these gentlemen might be, you won't.

Names have been changed to protect the identities of all concerned, whether they deserve it or not!

NICE GUYS ...
Or are they?!

THE IMPOSTER

Lisa decided she'd give online dating another whirl. After a string of failed relationships, she wanted to get back out into the world.

Her initial meet-up turned out to be with a guy she'd first chatted with for a whole month!!! Let's call him Dick.

> We've learned to chat for a few days, max, before meeting. You can't get a sense of a person until you're face-to-face, and you don't want to have too much time invested before you do!

Anyway, Lisa noticed that Dick was always available to text or chat and got back to her right away, day or night. It seemed a bit odd—never busy at work? Or anything? But maybe, she thought optimistically, he was just really, really into her. Awesome, right?!

He seemed to be doing okay. He told her he owned three companies and a house on one of the local lakes.

She was intrigued.

They finally decided to meet, and Lisa was pumped.

On the day of the date, he messaged to say his truck was in the shop and asked if she would mind picking him up at his house. No problem.

As she pulled up and spotted him waiting in the driveway, she panicked. This was NOT the guy in the photos, and he looked closer to 50 than the age he'd given in his profile (she was 20-something). He was COVERED in tattoos, like all the way up to his neck, and had a huge scar across his face. His hair was greasy, as if it had been a while since it saw a shower.

Honestly, in Lisa's view, he kinda looked like a total creep. The kind of guy you wouldn't want to meet alone on a dark street.

But she felt connected with him after a month of texting and so took a deep breath and got out of the car.

He asked her to come in, and after some brief small talk about the traffic, she asked him why he had a day off midweek. He told her he'd been laid off ... da fuck?!? When she reminded him of their conversation about his three companies, he admitted he didn't actually own them and hadn't worked IN A YEAR!!!

"Is this your place?" she asked.

"No, it's my buddy's," he said. "I'm just staying here."

Now Lisa was fuming at what was clearly a very extreme case of liar, liar pants on fire. But she was also freaking out ... I mean, what could she do? She's in his house (well, his friend's house) and walking out would be super uncomfortable.

So, she went for dinner with him. When they walked into the restaurant together, everyone stared, and not like they were Kanye and Kim. More like, "Should we call the cops?"

She felt totally awkward. To top off the night, her friend was waitressing at the restaurant and later asked, "What were you doing with that old guy?"

Thankfully the night ended without a police report, but not before Dick asked Lisa to swing by the liquor store before dropping him off at home. And since Lisa is a doll, she did just that.

When she got home, she took another look at his profile and verified that he had no tattoos in his photos. He looked completely different— yet his profile audaciously asked, "My pics are recent ... are yours?"

Lisa, we feel you. Way to tough it out!!! But next time, stay safe!

LESSONS LEARNED

1. If a guy won't meet you within the first two weeks, drop him. Your time is precious, girl!

2. Casually ask for some selfies by text before meeting. We recommend using terms like, "let's trade pics!" or "pic for a pic?" You might even go so far as to ask him to hold up today's newspaper.

3. When you pull up to meet a guy you've met online and he doesn't look like his profile pictures, keep driving. Maybe look around as if you are looking for parking, or like you didn't see him, and then get the hell out of there. Go!

THE LITIGANT

Becky met Alan online. He seemed like a great catch, and she was really into him right off the bat.

Things seemed to be going well, even though his personality lacked in a few areas. He didn't have the best sense of humour, and he was a little moody, but she was willing to see where it would go.

It was right around the three-month mark that he asked her if she wanted to go to New York with him in two months. Becky had been many times but it would be his first time, so she agreed to be his tour guide.

> *Becky asked us to add a side note: Alan has the smallest penis she has ever encountered, and she's a nurse, so she's seen thousands! She calls it a "micro-penis." Penis-lite. Penie.*
>
> *We digress, but it is important information.*

During the next two months, though, things changed, and Becky wasn't feeling it anymore. Literally. She'd lost her attraction to him— the initial spark was just gone. She slowly, regretfully came to the realization that she would hate being stuck on a plane with him, let alone in the Big Apple.

Her friends encouraged her to go anyway—it was a free trip to New York. But she knew she couldn't fake it and felt it wouldn't be fair to him to try. She expected him to be disappointed because she knew she would be had their roles been reversed.

Instead, he was furious. Rather than being upset because their connection hadn't worked out, he seemed to be completely focused on the fact that he didn't have trip cancellation insurance.

Becky felt bad but knew it wasn't really her issue. Sometimes things just don't work out.

Two weeks later, she was served with legal papers at work. Yes, Alan sued her for the cost of her portion of the trip. She couldn't believe it ... what a douche! It had been completely his idea to go, and he'd offered to pay.

She ended up settling through a mediator and paying part of the cost of the plane ticket.

LESSONS LEARNED

1. GET CANCELLATION INSURANCE WHEN BOOKING A FLIGHT IF IT'S A NEW RELATIONSHIP.

2. Be leery of a guy who offers to pay for a trip—is it a gift or a deal?

3. If a guy has a micro-penis and is not "Bradley-Fucking-Cooper"* or a National Level oral champion, just end it. It's not about the sex—millions of lesbians can't be wrong. It's about the insecurity and all the baggage that goes with it. A man who's angry at Mother Nature is never going to be happy.

*Hail to the Chief, Amy Schumer.

THE ANAL COMPULSIVE

Have you ever had a moment on a first date when you wanted to dig a hole and hide in it?

Jill has. If only she'd had a shovel ...

It all started as a blind date. She was set up by a friend at work who wanted Jill to meet her son. He picked her up on time (bonus points) and they went to a local pub.

Sam was attractive and had a sweet smile that made her tingle. Their conversation flowed, which seems to be a challenge too often these days. He had a terrific sense of humour and there were no awkward silences.

He reached across the table to casually touch her hand often. Then he paid for dinner, whipping out his wallet and graciously saying, "I'd like to get this if that's okay," before she even had time to go through the uncomfortable "Should I offer to pay half even though I only ate a quarter of the appetizer because I was trying to fake not being hungry?" mind-pretzel process that usually accompanies a first-date meal.

Since they both seemed to be feeling it, they extended the date and drove to the beach as the sun was setting. It was a beautiful evening. The sky was a maze of colour, the breeze kissed her bare shoulders, and his hand rested gently on the small of her back. She turned to him, gazed deep into his eyes, and watched his lips move, hoping he'd lean in for a kiss.

Instead, he asked, "Do you like anal?"

Um, shoot, what?

She gave an awkward smile, hoping he was going to laugh out loud any second. But nope, deadpan, not even a flinch. She had this horrible vision of his mom finding out about her and her anal tendencies.

She gracefully declined to answer the question, and the date ended pretty much right then and there; she figured it was no loss if a guy needs that particular information right off the bat.

You don't want to know my favourite colour first? Or whether I like kittens and puppies???

LESSONS LEARNED

1. Don't watch sunsets on the first date; apparently, certain men associate them with anal sex.

2. Don't go on a date with the son of someone you work with. You may find out things about their family that traumatize you forever.

3. If you're not a fan of anal, and someone catches you off guard with a question about your preferences, perhaps respond with, "I'm agnostic, but right now I have stomach cramps and a bit of diarrhea." We always like to go for the shock factor.

THE SLEEPWALKER

Sophia had a hard and fast rule: no dating guys she worked with. So while she was sorry to hear that her sexy co-worker Guy had been laid off, she could also see the bright side.

He had piercing blue eyes, hair that was always perfectly coiffed, broad shoulders, and he smelled like a million bucks. She'd been attracted to him for a while, so she knew she had to jump on the chance before someone else did.

A friend organized drinks and, knowing he'd be there, Sophia dressed to the nines. She curled her hair, put on long fake lashes, and bought a new lipstick shade she was sure could make any guy weak in the knees.

It was a hot summer night, and the booze flowed. It was a blast, and at one point Sophia started thinking she should probably leave things with Guy just as they were—friends.

Now, like most young women, Sophia likes to do shots occasionally when she's out on the town. And as with most young women, that either means things are gonna get messy or it's going to be an epic night.

When their mutual friend decided to head home, Sophia and Guy decided to keep drinking (maybe a mistake?) and then things got a tad fuzzy. You can imagine where they went from there, though.

They ended up at Sophia's place, and one thing led to another. Nothing memorable, she'd like to note, though admittedly, her memory wasn't working at full capacity at this point.

Afterwards, they both fell asleep, and at one point super-late in the night, or very early in the morning, whatever you would call it, Sophia heard Guy get up and use the washroom. There was a bunch of crashing around, but she was so out of it she soon fell back asleep.

She woke again an hour later to a sound so loud she almost shit her bed right then and there. A dark figure lurked in her doorway—it was the kind of scary movie scene where you cover your eyes.

But nothing attacked her, so she eventually found the courage to get up and investigate. Looking closer, she realized the strange dark mass was ... her coat rack?! Some of the coats were still on it, but most were on the floor. "What the fuck!" she thought. Glancing back at her bed, she realized Guy wasn't in it. Okay, what was happening here?

The living room looked as if a tornado had swept through. The missing coats were all over the floor, along with the contents of a drawer. Her Christmas wreath was on a chair in the corner of the room.

This was wrong on so many levels.

One of the many misplaced items from the drawer, a large box of craft supplies, was chilling on the coffee table.

And there was Guy, laying naked on Sophia's couch, hugging her very expensive Mongolian accent pillow to his sweaty bits. He resembled a pale, hairless cat.

For a minute or two, she just watched him snore, blissfully unaware of the mess he'd made. When her heart rate slowed to normal, she covered him with a blanket, as the apartment was freezing, and went back to bed.

A couple of hours later, she had to awkwardly wake him, hand him his clothes, and drive him home.

A few days after, Guy called to see how things were with her and explained he'd never slept with a close friend before. He then asked if he'd upset her that night because he remembered waking up on the couch—he assumed she'd kicked him out of her room.

She explained everything that had happened, and he had no recollection at all. Shockingly, they haven't talked much since then.

LESSONS LEARNED

1. When you meet a guy, casually ask questions like, "Oh btw, do you have any major sleeping disorders?" or, "What are your thoughts on accent pillows?" Awkward, but it could save you from the experience of your own middle-of-the-night horror story and/or provide you with a home decor shopping partner.

2. There's absolutely nothing wrong with handcuffing a guy to the bed, for sexual and safety reasons. Just make sure the key is somewhere you can find it—we all know these guys need to be gone early the next day!

THE LATE-TO-LAUNCH OUTLAW

Jordy and Linda connected online—it was a swipe-right sort of thing.

He had an appealing write-up, and she was drawn to his look. Tall and stocky, he was the kind of guy who could give you the best bear hug while making you feel tiny and safe no matter how tall you are.

It didn't take him three days to message her back; he could write full sentences and scored an 8/10 on Linda's "grammar police" scale.

> *It is amazing how many guys struggle with "your" and "you're." I mean, we all make mistakes when we're texting, but it can be hard to take a man seriously when he can't or doesn't bother to maintain elementary school-level grammar and spelling, even for his profile!*

They decided to meet for dinner and he offered to pick her up, as he lived close by. He pulled up in a gorgeous, brand new blue truck. It was the kind that was so lifted that, had she been wearing a dress, it would have been Paris Hilton and Britney Spears climbing out of a limo all over again, only with a thong. She managed to hoist herself up and was welcomed by a pleasant aroma of cologne. It was subtle, not overwhelming, and so enticing she immediately had goosebumps.

He seemed shy and scared to look into her eyes. She tried to make the most of the ride to the restaurant, making idle chitchat and complimenting his truck (might as well build up his ego a little). They got to the restaurant and found a seat in the corner.

The conversation felt a little awkward. She struggled to find things to ask, and he was apparently feeling the same way.

The waitress arrived at the perfect time, cutting their uncomfortable interview-like conversation short. They ordered food and Linda's first red flag was that he asked for no vegetables. When she asked him about it, he said he hated fruits and vegetables and therefore never ate them.

She thought this was kind of crazy—how do you avoid fruits and vegetables entirely? Maybe she should have let it go, but she was so curious. She asked if he'd have a smoothie, you know, the yummy ones with the berries and stuff, or even a juice smoothie. Nope, no, he would not.

Spinach dip? She was shut down again. She asked about veggie lasagna, no go. He said he eats lasagna, but only with meat, cheese and pasta. He said eating vegetables made him gag.

He then proceeded to tell her that he stopped at McDonald's every morning on the way home from work after his nightshifts—so basically, he was a heart attack waiting to happen.

The next doozie was the fact that, at 35, he lived with his parents. AND his mom did all of the cooking AND his laundry. No wonder he could buy a $70,000 truck.

The next fun fact she found out was that he'd never gone to the dentist in his twenties, so now had to have thousands of dollars' worth of work done on his teeth. As far as health and self-care went, Jordy was turning out to be less a fixer-upper than a tear-down.

The conversation lightened a bit as they moved on to talk about travel and where they each wanted to go. Linda told him about her love of Disneyland and asked if he'd ever been. It was then that he put his head down, minimizing eye contact even more, and told her he'd been arrested in the United States for fighting and was no longer able to cross the border. WHAT??!! How was she ever going to get Annie's Pretzels with him? Or Applebee's? Or go to Disneyland? IT'S THE HAPPIEST PLACE ON EARTH, FOR FUCK SAKES!

Linda is not one to judge. She felt terrible for the guy, as we've all made mistakes. It's just that this one would follow him around for a while! She sadly watched him eat his mac and cheese, so tempted to throw a piece of lettuce or a sprinkle of green onions on there to see what would happen.

She was open to dating guys who may not check off many of the items on her wish list, and that list had been tweaked many times over the years. She had a higher bar when she was younger, but now she just wanted a guy with a great personality, nice teeth, a cute ass, a career and a pulse. She might have been able to deal with Jordy's criminal record—it was kinda sexy in a way. But "Mommy washes my tighty whities?" "No fruits or vegetables?"

It was all too much for her.

She moved on—to a man who ate leafy green vegetables and could use a washing machine and travel across borders with her.

LESSONS LEARNED

1. Fruits and vegetables are good for you. McDonald's every day is bad. (Don't tell us you didn't learn anything from reading this book ... this is your take-home message.) Also, just not sexy.

2. A guy that drives a $70,000 truck and lives with his parents isn't worth your time. (Sorry, guys!!! But really, grow up. You owe it to yourself.)

3. Ask for a criminal record prior to meeting up. If the criminal activity keeps you from travelling to other countries, you've got some things to think about. Disneyland ... right???

THE PROUD
PENNY-PINCHER

Judy was a nurse by profession, and deep down, she felt that it takes a very special person to be a nurse.

If you're a nurse and you're reading this, we salute you!

When she met fellow nurse Rod online, she thought, "Perfect, maybe he'll understand me." She figured she'd be able to be her disgusting self and he'd be okay with it. Well, he was. They could joke about poop and yeast infections and still had chemistry at the end of the day. Sounds like a dream guy right!?!

Well, let's not jump too far ahead. We'll discuss their first date and go from there.

She suggested a higher-end coffee shop because she's into fancy lattes and shit like that. He, however, wanted to meet at your standard, run-of-the-mill coffee shop, so she agreed. As she walked in, she let out the breath she'd been holding, because he actually looked like his pictures.

He was cute and super funny. Everyone appreciates good banter, and he gave her a run for her money! He could dish it out and take it, and she liked it.

They were in line for coffee, and when the young lady at the counter called them up to order, she thought Rod would just ask her what she wanted, but then it got awkward. He pushed ahead of her and went up alone. Judy wasn't sure if she was supposed to follow him or just wait until it was her turn. Briefly paralyzed, she thought, "The coffee here is less than two dollars, and he invited me. I'm sure he can spring for it." So she boldly went up and stood beside him at the till. He still didn't ask what she wanted, so she just ordered a coffee and he basically had no choice but to pay for both.

They found a booth in the corner and sat down across from one another. They seemed to have a lot in common; they both liked the outdoors, travelling, their jobs and coffee! As the conversation continued, Judy was pleasantly surprised that they seemed to want the same things as well. They were both looking for a long-term relationship and hoped to have kids and a dog one day along with a white picket fence (although she did love seafoam blue). It was refreshing to talk to somebody who understood the ins and outs of nursing and how stressful and emotionally draining it could be.

At the end of the date, he hugged her goodbye and asked if she'd like to see a movie the following day. She almost fell over. It's very rare to have a guy end the date by organizing another date—she liked it! She agreed to a movie and he said he would get tickets.

Later that evening he texted to tell her he bought the tickets and even sprang for the IMAX 3D!!! Amazing! She thanked him and told him she was excited, and then she watched and waited as the little text bubble (you know, that one with the three dots that tells you someone is typing) floated for a few moments.

Apparently, it's called an ellipsis. Megan calls them Lypsils.

The next text that arrived said she owed him $20. Um, okay, really? She wasn't sure if he was joking or not; she'd never actually had a guy pay for something and then tell her that she owed him money.

After pausing for a moment, she texted, "Thanks, no worries. I'll give you some money tomorrow." She waited for him to text back with, "Just kidding! Why don't you just get the next one?" but there was ellipsis silence, and she was just left looking at her phone with a weird feeling in her stomach.

> *We understand it's tough nowadays—I mean, who pays for what? Do we split everything? Who knows? It's so confusing, and it stresses us out!*

Anyway, they met at the movie the next day. She handed over the crisp, $20 bill she'd brought along for the occasion and he tucked it into his pocket.

This was the first of a few odd moments that Judy would question, but she put it behind her and they took their seats in the theatre. They had a great time at the movie, so they decided to continue the date by grabbing a coffee at the quaint little place next door. He ordered a pop (or soda, if that's your thing) and she ordered a coffee. They continued on with their conversation, laughing and bantering back and forth.

After an hour or so, the waitress dropped off the bill. Judy could see from where she was sitting that it was $6.28. It sat there, the elephant in the room. It seemed to be directly in the centre of the table, no closer to him, no closer to her. But she was sure he would definitely offer to pay. A date was a date.

He was gainfully employed, and she even knew how much money he made per hour (the downside of working in the same industry). Given they probably earned close to the same income, she didn't expect him to shoulder more than his fair share of dating expenses—on the other hand, she'd been raised to understand that, when you ask someone out, you're offering a gift. She was looking forward to responding in kind at some point in the future, but it now felt she was involved in some kind of stand-off.

Minutes ticked by, and the conversation started to become awkward. Judy finally had to leave, so she reached down for her wallet, and he seemed to do the same. They awkwardly fumbled around for a bit, until Judy gave in and finally threw down cash and said, "I got this." He said thanks, and he watched as she left a tip for the waitress. That's when he dropped the other red flag bomb.

"I don't tip," he said.

Judy felt her neck snap as she whipped her head up so that her eyes could meet his. Um, excuse me, what? Like ever? Never? No, he didn't tip. He said it was "the principle." He shouldn't have to give money to people who made less than him just for doing their jobs.

"I don't get paid extra to care for patients, why should I tip?"

This was bad. Judy wasn't even really sure how to respond. She had friends in the service industry, and they busted their asses on the daily for something like nothing per hour, plus they put up with hungry, cranky people! She told him she completely disagreed and became quite defensive. They finally stood and walked out of the café. She was a bit shocked when, after the tense moments inside, he asked her out again.

She's not sure why, but she said sure. It's always been her "principle" to give a guy a few chances to win her heart. He invited her to his place for a movie the following day. She agreed, but she did wonder if he would ask her to pay for half the movie rental.

The next evening, Judy left work and headed to his place. She texted to ask if he had any wine as she thought it would be nice to have a glass while watching the movie. He said he didn't and asked her to pick up a bottle. He offered to pay for half. Okay, WTF, really? He couldn't even run out to get a bottle of wine when a woman was coming over?

There was no point in putting up a fight, though. When she got to his house, he didn't offer any money for the wine, not that she was surprised. Since it had been a while for Judy, and she'd had some wine, they ended up hooking up that night. It was decent. But not mind-blowing. Definitely not "You've made me forget you don't tip" great.

In the days that followed, they continued to chat on and off, but Judy was pretty clear that they had very different values.

On their next date, he made a comment about how much money she must make, since she'd been a nurse for 15 years, and asked if she'd be his sugar mama. That wasn't the only time he pulled that shit. She looked at her online banking one day when she was with him and realized a payment had come out unexpectedly; she'd forgotten to cancel something. He told her not to worry because she was rich; she made more money than him.

To Judy, it seemed super tacky to make comments about a person's income right off the bat. Are they doing it because of their own confidence issues, or are they intimidated? Either way, it's a major turn off.

> *By the way, if you purchased this book, thanks for helping us reach our goal of "rich," whatever that may mean nowadays!*

The boiling point for Judy wasn't about money or lack of willingness to spend thereof. She'd had a knee injury and was really disappointed to miss cycling in an upcoming charity event she'd been looking forward to. When she mentioned how bummed she was to Rod, he told her she shouldn't have begged him for sex, and maybe that was how she injured it. So much for tea and sympathy.

> *Why is it such a struggle for some guys to have serious conversations and not bring their dick into the matter? Do they literally think about sex all day every day? Grow up! Here's a tip: girls will think it's hotter if you're attentive and listen to them. They will, therefore, be more likely to have sex with you.*
>
> *If you're a guy and this section of the book gets you laid, you're welcome!*

Regardless of all they had in common, and all the laughs they had, it was time to cut ties with cheapskate Rod. It's one thing to not even offer to buy a girl a coffee but to make a bad joke when she's having a tough time is just not cool.

LESSONS LEARNED

1. A guy should buy you a coffee on a first date. Simple. Some may disagree, but it's a coffee, for crying out loud!

2. If you can't have a serious conversation with a guy, break it off. Life is challenging, and you deserve someone who will listen to and support you.

MR. "IS IT IN?"

Beth met Adam, you guessed it, online. He was super cute and lived nearby, which was a bonus.

> All the good guys seem to live 40 miles away—ain't no girl got time for drivin' that far!

They went on a couple of dates, mostly for drinks, and hit it off. He was a little quiet and shy, but as time went on he started to be more comfortable around her, and they had a lot of laughs.

He rented a basement suite, worked as an arborist (if you need to look up that word, it's okay, Beth did the same), and seemed pretty normal (whatever "normal" is).

After a few dates, they ended up back at his place. They decided to watch a movie, which, in Beth's past experience, usually leads to sex.

> Although sometimes you really just want to watch the movie without a guy trying to penetrate you. We especially want to watch the movie if there's a hot guy or a cute puppy in it, and if it has both you better keep away until the end credits roll.

Anyway, things got hot and heavy, and they ended up on the bed in an intense make-out session. He was a little shy in this department, and Beth had to take the lead a few times, which she was totally willing to do on occasion! As things progressed, they ended up naked on the bed and Beth was ready for what she thought of as big daddy time.

> *Ewww, that actually sounds gross.*

He was on top of her, breathing heavy, eyes clenched shut, when he got an odd look on his face. She realized he'd climaxed—and she hadn't felt a thing!!!

He ended up enjoying himself immensely; she was left unsatisfied and confused.

> *On a side note, we recently went to a sex toy party with some girlfriends, and they have some penis extender things that we never knew existed!!!*

As nice as he was, and as much as she felt bad for the poor guy, she needed a little more "something" in the bedroom. A lot more actually!

LESSONS
LEARNED

1. Not every penis is going to be perfect. Hopefully, the guy attached to it IS, at least to you. Either way, you don't have to accept what nature gave you—there are plenty of "apps" out there that can make a woman scream in the nicest possible way.

2. Don't ever say "big daddy." Just don't.

DJ DOUCHE

A local DJ Nat had known for a while and occasionally worked with asked her out on a date.

Now Nat always believed in the "don't shit where you eat," adage, so she thought twice before committing to the date but finally decided to go for it. She'd been single for a while, and although she was feeling okay about the lack of texts she was receiving from the opposite sex, she was also starting to crave a little male attention.

Thom was the most Rico Suave guy she'd had ever met, and she usually hated those guys. They were often (aka always) full of shit— but what harm could come from one date?

Nat and her friends decided to show up at the club he was working at a week before the scheduled date. He treated them so well—he bought them drinks and couldn't stop telling Nat's friends how much he liked her. It was a little over the top, but again, it was nice to have the attention.

> *It should have been a warning sign, really. If something feels way too fake, it's probably way too fake.*

When they left the club a while later, he started texting her OFF THE HOOK, asking if he could meet up with her. At that point, Nat and her friend had just taken a seat in the local Denny's and ordered the greasiest plate of food on the menu. She realized her breath could have killed a small village, and the animals within that village, as well as some people on the outskirts of that small village. So she asked Thom if he could meet up the next night.

It was a weekend, and the girls met up the following afternoon and started a little day drinking despite being completely hungover from the previous night.

> *We've all been there. No judgement.*

Thom texted Nat and said he'd be in the area and wanted to pop by to say hi to her and her friends. When he pulled up, Nat ran out, chatted for a few minutes, stole a quick kiss, and joined her friends back in the bar. Even though he wasn't her type, when she saw him that day she had a few little butterflies fluttering around inside.

> *Ugh, we hate it when this happens—because it always seems to happen with the wrong guys, are we right??*

Nat and the girls (stupidly) decided to continue their day drinking and met up at another venue where Thom was working that evening. They ended up getting completely annihilated and the girls cabbed it home, leaving Nat to make a choice: go home or go with Thom?

Well, you guessed it, she and Thom ended up back at her place. They both continued to drink, which led to some pretty average sex, nothing memorable. But hey, sometimes we gotta take what we can get!

Over the next week, he texted her every day. They decided to go on another date towards the end of the week. Well, this is when Mr. Rico Suave came out in full force. He took her to a really swanky restaurant. When they were seated, he made a point of ordering a very special bottle of wine, ordered her food for her and stood when she got up to use the restroom. (How gentleman-like!)

He even insisted on ordering dessert (although she'd tried to be the typical skinny woman and refused) and proceeded to feed it to her.

Dream guy?! Thankfully he didn't do little airplane or train sounds—though it would have added additional pizazz to this story.

After dessert, they left the restaurant and went back to his house. They listened to music, drank wine and then attempted another "session." Thankfully it was better this time, though Nat still cringes when she tells this story. When all was said and done, it was about 2 a.m. Nat thought they were going to lie there and chill, but instead, he got up, looked at his phone, and said, "I have to go."

Keep in mind that they were at HIS house. She didn't really know what to do—this had never happened to her before. Go home? Stay? She finally said, "Where are you going?" His response was, "I just have to go."

She thought he'd be gone for a few minutes, half an hour tops, so she said she would just stay and sleep. When she thinks back, yes, that was dumb. She should have just gone home. But she worked early the next morning, and he lived just steps from her place of employment, so she figured she'd just try and sleep a bit.

At 7:30 a.m., Nat woke up to the sound of Thom coming into his apartment. She couldn't really think of what to say, so she blurted out, "How was your night?" to which he just responded, "Good."

He gave her a kiss, wrapped his arms around her and proceeded to fall asleep like nothing had happened. Nat left for work a short while later, leaving him a little note saying goodbye and thanks for the evening.

That day she kept wondering to herself, "Where the fuck did he go for five hours?"

She would never find out. They texted randomly here and there after that, but nothing ever really amounted to a third date. After the week of incessant texts and attention, it was over.

Nat made up all of these scenarios in her head: maybe he had a wife and kid he had to check on? Maybe he was in the mafia? A drug dealer? Maybe he had to go and feed the homeless? Maybe he had diarrhea and didn't want to shit in the same house as her? Maybe he'd already shit his pants?

To this day, she still wonders, but it will always remain a mystery.

LESSONS LEARNED

1. Never date a DJ, period. Or a comedian. (There is a whole other Und8ables book that could be written about this.)

2. Sex is not like wine. If it sucks, it won't automatically get better over time. (We still have faith that it can improve with the right training, but he needs to be trainable.)

3. If a guy leaves you alone in his house for more than 60 minutes, take it as a clear sign he's not husband material. Unless he comes back with a diamond ring, poutine with extra cheese and maybe a puppy.

GO WITH YOUR GUT, GIRL

Dalia took us on a journey back to her high-school days to one of her first serious relationships, with a guy who tested her female intuition and her detective skills as well.

She started dating Tommy just before prom and things were going well, so she thought it was pretty odd when he told her he'd be taking another girl, Jane. His reason was that he had agreed to do so months before and it was too late to change the plan.

Dalia went to prom with her friends, but she had a queasy "something doesn't feel right" pang in her stomach. She brushed it off and Tommy did spend time with her that evening. She was excited to go to the post-prom party with him. At the party, they mingled with their friends, snuck a few alcoholic beverages when the parents weren't looking and gossiped like high-schoolers do.

Towards the end of the evening, though, she saw Tommy talking intently to Jane. When he led her upstairs, Dalia felt her face and neck flush with anger.

She didn't see him again until the next day, when she confronted him about his disappearance. He said that nothing had happened and she was overreacting.

> *Whenever a man says a woman is overreacting, it's a good bet there is probably something going on. And it's not something she's going to like.*

As people do when they're young and in love, however, Dalia chose to believe him.

Shortly after graduation, she moved about four hours away for school. She and Tommy promised to make their relationship work even though it would be long distance. They dated for about two years, and towards the end of the second year, Dalia had that "something isn't right" feeling again.

Too many of Tommy's social media photos included another girl. There were no public displays of affection—it was nothing crazy—but it gave Dalia the same feeling she'd felt years before during graduation.

She decided she'd put her feelings to the test, and called Tommy's best friend. She casually mentioned she knew Tommy was fooling around with another girl, and that everyone was talking about it. Well, wouldn't you know, he fell for it! He went on to say that he was surprised too, and that he thought Tommy was an idiot for trying to hide it, and that everyone knew. Oh wow, so everyone really DID know! Everyone except Dalia. She wanted to hit him where it hurt, so she called his mom and told her what was happening, and his mom drove to the girl's house to confront them both. Tommy was humiliated and that was good enough for Dalia.

She decided to move on. Afterward, she learned that Tommy had slept with at least seven other women during their relationship, so she got herself swabbed for every STI in the book and never spoke to him again.

Here's where things get more complicated. The girl Tommy cheated with who appeared in his social media photos had recently broken up with her boyfriend, Chad. Dalia and Chad connected over this scandalous cheating episode and ended up dating a few months later. They soon moved in together. Long story short, it didn't go well, but they met Tim, a neighbour across the alley. After Chad and Dalia broke up, Tim continued to invite her over for drinks and barbeques. She wasn't interested in Tim romantically at first, but over time, she realized he was an amazingly caring, thoughtful guy.

One evening, after a few too many cocktails, they ended up hooking up.

That was 11 years ago, and they're now married with two beautiful kids. They couldn't be happier. Dalia is inexpressibly grateful to Tommy for being such a lying cheat that she ended up with Chad, and to Chad for—well, that's a long story, but let's just say—clearing the field for Tim.

They were so happy together they didn't plan on getting married. Why change anything when everything is perfect? It just worked.

Two years later, they were ecstatic when their first daughter arrived. But in the long discussion about whose last name the baby should have, they decided to get married and exchanged vows three days later in their living room. It all happened so fast that Dalia didn't have time to get a dress, so she wore the outfit in which she looked most herself—and therefore most beautiful—nice jeans and a white t-shirt.

Yes, sometimes there is a happy ending, even in a book full of bad dates. We hope you'll think of Dalia's story when you realize you're with a Tommy or a Chad. Your Tim might be right across the alley.

LESSONS LEARNED

1. Never settle! There IS someone amazing out there for you. In fact, he may be just a few yards away—don't give up just before he finally decides to wander over and say "howdy."

2. Give the guys who may not be "your type" a chance. (Remember that the guys who are your type haven't exactly delivered for you in the past, right?) Our prerequisite list needs to be tweaked now and then; we change and so should our wants and needs.

MEN WITH ISSUES ...
So many issues.

RUDE AWAKENING(S)

In her 20s, Jane didn't date guys with kids; it just wasn't for her. She'd always known she wanted her own; she just wasn't sure she'd be good at helping to raise someone else's. That said, as she entered her late 30s, she decided she could really be missing out on someone wonderful. A lot of her friends were in relationships with men who had children from a previous relationship, and they'd found happiness.

Plus, there's something irresistible about a dad who is super sexy!!! Right?!?

So, when Kevin, a father of two, messaged her, Jane decided that a coffee date couldn't hurt. He seemed really funny and easy to chat with, and he sounded like an excellent dad, so bonus points for him!

He'd been a police officer for many years, and on their first date, he mentioned how he'd "seen a lot" and sometimes had trouble sleeping.

As a nurse, Jane could relate. She'd witnessed some difficult things that were hard to forget, so she understood where he was coming from.

Kevin was also really big into working out. (His body was amazing!) He drank a lot of energy drinks, many of them containing caffeine, so he was wired all the time.

Their first couple of dates consisted of dinner and drinks, and Jane found she really enjoyed his company (and his body). But she had the feeling he had some deep dark demons that he was battling, perhaps from his past relationships, or perhaps from his job. There were many things he wouldn't talk about or seemed to shy away from when she asked about them, so she just let them go.

On their third date, they ended up back at his house, and one thing led to another. They ended up doing the horizontal mambo; laughing, chatting, cuddling and generally just having a great time. As they fell asleep, he held her tightly against him. Now, she was all for cuddling, but after a few minutes, she needed space to move around!

When she told him this, he seemed a little upset and letdown, but she didn't really think anything of it. She must have fallen asleep because she was awakened suddenly by a hand shaking her shoulder and a dark shadow looming over the bed.

She sat up, thinking there was an emergency, and said, "What's wrong?" Was there a fire? Had he hurt himself?

His response? "I'm cooking up a storm downstairs."

Jane was so confused. Had this guy actually just woken her at 2:30 in the morning to tell her that he was cooking?

She thought everyone knew that you don't wake nurses up, ever, unless there's a fire or someone is dying. She told him he'd woken her out of a dead sleep and that she wasn't getting out of bed. He left the room, mumbling something, and she got the feeling he was pissed off she wouldn't join him. But after calming down from her initial panic, she turned over and fell back asleep.

Not long after, he woke her a second time. This time he was on the phone with a friend, laughing and chatting about a trip he was going on.

"Um, okay really??? Don't you ever sleep?" she thought to herself. "There is a naked woman up here in your bed and you're downstairs making wraps and talking to your homie!"

She was exhausted and pissed off, so she got up, got dressed and headed for the front door.

When Kevin saw her putting on her shoes, he hung up the phone and asked what was wrong.

"People gotta sleep," she said. "Just because you don't doesn't mean we're all like that."

She drove home and passed out on her bed. The next day Kevin messaged to ask her what was wrong and again wondered why she'd left. Jane explained how she felt being woken up twice was not cool, and he apologized, saying he should have realized that she needed her sleep. (Um ya, we all do!)

They dated for a little while but ended up drifting apart for numerous reasons—and now "must like sleep" is a prerequisite Jane looks for in a guy.

LESSONS LEARNED

1. It's not just nurses—as much as women love food, we like sleep more. Unless we wake up with food on the pillow beside us, and sometimes not even then.

2. A guy who passes up sleeping beside a beautiful naked woman in favour of a sandwich is not to be trusted.

3. A guy who passes up sleeping beside a naked woman to talk to his buddy while making sandwiches is not to be trusted.

THE PERSIAN PRINCE

Malea celebrated her 30th birthday last year on a fabulous night out with friends. She had no intention of getting with a guy; she'd been good and single for the previous few months. That said, as she got a drink at the bar of her favourite club, she glanced to her right and saw a tall drink of water all decked out in a suit, with nice shoes and perfect hair. And that face, my God, that face. Amir was a gorgeous Persian, and she was immediately hooked on him. Like, instantly. Like, hooked.

In retrospect, she should have seen the warning signs that night. He had a random freak-out after she talked on the phone to her friend Richard, who had called to see where she was heading later.

Malea decided to look past it.

> Yes, "decided to look past it" is a theme in this book.

He was just so hot. She couldn't remember the last time she'd had that sort of instant, intense attraction for someone. They ended up exchanging numbers and saw each other daily over the next week.

No amount of time seemed like enough with him, and the worst part was that she was leaving for England the following week for two weeks. She'd been so excited about her trip, but now she didn't want to go. Oh well, the flight was booked! If he was right for her, she told herself, he'd wait for her return.

Before she left, he asked Malea to promise him she wouldn't have sex with anyone while she was away. It seemed a little early, and she hesitated, but she was flattered, too. He wanted her all to himself! Before her flight took off, she texted to make the promise he'd asked for. She was staying with family anyway, so how hard could it be?! She was all in.

She assumed he'd do the same—that's how things work, right?

Two weeks later, he was there to pick her up at the airport, as gorgeous as ever.

It wasn't long, though, before Dr. Jekyll started showing his Mr. Hyde side. One of her friends passed away, and while Malea cried, his only response was, "Why are you crying?" (aka "This is bringing me down, sweetheart!")

He criticized her for having wine after work a couple of nights a week, yet he went out with friends to get obliterated every weekend, "forgetting" to text or call her all night or even for the entire weekend.

On social media, she found a video of him pouring vodka all over himself in someone's pool. He started ditching her for his friends.

She invited him for dinner at a restaurant with an amazing view of the city, and he seemed to be looking forward to it. She was so excited to spend a nice evening with him that she had butterflies and was all nervous. He had spent the weekend before away partying with his friends, so this was her chance for some alone-time with him.

He never showed up.

Classy!

The finale came one night when he ditched Malea for his friends yet again. After cancelling a date with her because he was tired and wanted to "just watch a movie at home," she watched his social media videos for the night and realized he'd partied until three-ish and then moved on to an after-party—on a Sunday night.

When 5 a.m. rolled around, she was up for work, and he called to ask if he could sleep at her place. She heard him telling the cab driver that he was on the phone with his "wife."

Um, ya right buddy, in your dreams!

He showed up at her door and proceeded to pass out drunk on her bed. Then Malea noticed a text banner pop up on his phone with a message from "Andrea."

The message read, "How could you do this to me?"

Unfortunately for him, he had drunkenly told Malea his iPhone password, so she typed it in to see what dirty deeds he had been up to.

It turns out that he'd been with Andrea a few hours before. At this point, Malea didn't even care. She took down Andrea's phone number, went into another room and called her. Andrea told her that she and Amir had been hanging out and had kissed. Then, apparently, he'd been kicked out of the party for being a douche. (Go figure.)

Since Malea had the phone open, she decided to check out a few other things. He'd given his number to yet another random girl earlier that night and was bombarding her with text messages about where they should meet up at 3 a.m. He'd told an ex-girlfriend he wanted to have sex with her. He was also meeting up with girls after he dropped Malea off at work, and was getting another girl to call him Big Boss Daddy.

> We think there were definitely some self-confidence issues, since not only was he not a boss, but Malea reports he definitely wasn't big, if you get our drift.

She woke up the lying little prick (see what we did there?) and told him what she had found. She was done. No one, and we mean no one, is that good-looking.

LESSONS LEARNED

1. As much as we'd like to think someone is our dream guy after a week of hanging out, things change. Take the time to get to know them and don't put all your eggs in one basket!

2. If you ever feel the need to go into your guy's phone to figure out what he's been up to, it's already over. Either you have trust issues, or he's a super-douche. Or both. Whatever the case, move on. There's no going back from here.

"DO NOT FUCKING GO DOWN THERE!"

A friend of ours had her first online dating experience at the age of 29. Erica had recently moved to a new city and wanted to check out the dude situation. What better way to meet some single men than a free online dating site where everyone is completely honest about who they are and how they look—right?!

So she started chatting with a man she met online within the first couple of weeks of living in the big city. His profile caught her eye: he was attractive, 5'9" (she's 5' 1"), had an intriguing career (he owned an antique store), loved to be active and seemed to be a good communicator.

After a few days of chatting and texting, they decided to meet. Gary invited her to meet him at his store and head out for a bite to eat from there. She found it and noticed an older gentleman hanging around out front. As she got out of her car and made her way over, she realized that this older, shorter, chubbier, balding man was Gary. He was about 5'2" and appeared to be about 10 years older than his profile pictures.

She had that sick feeling in her stomach—now what?! After greeting her like he was sure she wouldn't notice the vast difference between him and his online persona, he invited her inside to have a look around.

The stale cigarette stench was overwhelming, barely drowning out the unmistakable musty thrift store smell. It was packed floor to ceiling, so Erica had to weave and dodge her way around old knickknacks and furniture. She felt like she was being watched, and she was—deer heads and a stuffed bobcat stared at her from the walls and a dark corner.

After the tour of the store, he led her through a doorway near the back. It was his home! He lived on the other side of the store, and she found herself suddenly standing in his living room. It was filled with granny-like, faded floral furniture, and a television that had a dial on it ... a dial!!! The one thing she clearly recalls is that there were no windows and therefore no natural light whatsoever.

He offered her a glass of wine, which of course she accepted. (At this point, she would have preferred to chug the whole bottle.) As she put it to her lips, she saw that the glass was unwashed, with hardened food particles on the rim. She immediately put it down.

As he continued to give her the grand tour, she felt unsettled. It was very dark and stuffy. He asked if she wanted to check out his games room. Why not? But he opened an old door to a set of dirty stairs heading down into an even more dimly lit basement. Erica had that screaming "no, no, no, no, no!" feeling in her stomach.

> *Yes, this is the scene in a scary movie where viewers are yelling, "Are you an idiot? Why would you even go down there?" Thankfully, Erica must have heard them in the back of her mind.*

She backed away from the stairs and told Gary that she was starving and would rather just get a bite to eat. Thankfully, he agreed, and they left the horror movie set to go to dinner.

At dinner, the conversation spiralled downward. They talked about what they liked to do in their spare time; when Erica mentioned her love of the gym, Gary said working out was stupid and a waste of time—he'd rather be out in the wilderness. Erica didn't make a comeback. She could see from the way his stomach was hanging over his pants that he didn't live an active lifestyle of any description.

They decided to share a platter of appetizers, and when the waitress informed them that they were out of dry ribs, Gary became an arrogant prick, laying on his dissatisfaction pretty thick.

When the bill came, he insisted on paying, though Erica pushed to pay for her share, hoping to signal that this date would go no further.

As they left the table, Erica could see he hadn't tipped the waitress. She worked in the service industry and wouldn't stand for this lack of respect, so she quickly threw a $10 bill on the table while Gary had his back turned.

Erica called a friend to come and pick her up, rather hastily, and hoped Gary would just leave. But no—he insisted on waiting with her. It was an awkward few minutes. Erica's friend pulled up (she had never been so happy to see her) and Gary reached out for a hug, which Erica uncomfortably obliged with a quick pat on the back.

To close, Erica's first online dating experience was a huge musty-smelling dud, but that didn't stop her from getting back on the horse (or the antique stuffed bobcat) and trying again.

LESSONS LEARNED

1. During the texting phase, ask for a photo of him standing by a newly installed local landmark that will allow you to assess his height. Tell him it's just your "thing."

2. Never ever, ever, ever go in the basement. This goes double if there are taxidermy animals on the wall.

3. If a guy wants a hug at the end of the date, and you're not feeling it, pull a casual side hug, or tell him you have personal space issues. He doesn't deserve to feel your boobs pressed up against him in any way, shape or form.

4. We've said this before, but if he doesn't look like his photos, just keep driving. If you're on foot, tell him you just came by to tell him in person you have to change plans. Skedaddle. Anything that starts this badly is going to get worse.

JUST BACK IT UP A BIT, MISTER.

Have you ever been on a date that ends up including some of the most uncomfortable moments of your life? Our friend Karen has!

She met Jim online, and it would go down in history as one of her worst dates ever. They decided to meet for a drink at a local restaurant, which is always a safe move in the online dating world. Nobody wants to be stuck on a long dinner date, or in a place they can't escape, or, heaven forbid, out in a kayak on the ocean. (Been there, done that.)

She met him just inside the doors and he was not not attractive. Let's call him semi-attractive—not exactly what she expected based on his photos and his description of himself. But he was chatty right off the bat, which Karen liked. The hostess sat them at a table with a bar stool and a bench, so Karen politely sat on the stool, thinking he might like the bench. Instead of taking his seat, Jim stole another bar stool from the table beside them and placed it directly next to Karen. Now, when we say next, we mean his knees were on either side of her knees.

Karen was unsure what to do here. I mean, can we establish some boundaries right off the bat? Like, can you get off me?

As the conversation progressed, Jim seemed to become even more comfortable with Karen, because he leaned in even closer to her ... and closer, and closer. Each time he leaned in, Karen had to lean back. It was just too much! It got to the point that she had to get up and stand beside the table to avoid falling backwards off her stool.

She stood there, sweetly, continuing the conversation from beside her stool, because she's just like that. She wasn't sure if he was leaning in to try to kiss her, or whether he just really liked to talk closely. Perhaps she had great breath?

She opted for date number two, thinking that he might have just been really nervous. Everyone deserves a second chance, right?

They met for another drink, this time at a table that had three stools. She cleverly waited for Jim to sit down and then sat directly across from him—and what did he do? He got up and moved, right next to her! That's when the leaning started again, and this time, Karen couldn't even get a word in edgewise. He leaned and talked, talked and leaned, completely oblivious to the fact that she was leaning so far back she was in danger of falling and hadn't said a word since they'd sat down.

She just couldn't do it. She downed her drink as quickly as she could without actually chugging and told him she had to get going, as she had to wake up the next morning.

> *Now, read that again: she told him she had to wake up the next morning. (If we could insert a laughing emoji here we would!) I mean, who **DOESN'T** have to wake up in the morning???!!!*
>
> *We're definitely keeping that one in our pocket for future emergencies!*

Needless to say, Jim didn't get date number three, OR a kiss. Just a lot of Karen's hot breath (which we hope was not minty fresh).

LESSONS LEARNED

1. When on a date, try to choose a booth, preferably one of the small ones with a single seat on either side. They're usually stationary, so he'll have no choice but to sit across from you.

2. If you're into him, you'll want to maintain fresh breath. If you're not, and especially if he is in your personal space, go for the meal with the most garlic. And ask for extra garlic.

IS SILENCE GOLDEN, REALLY?

Our friend Beth went on a series of dates with guys she met online. Some good, some bad—some awkward and forgettable, some memorable enough we can include them here.

Now, Beth can strike up a conversation with almost anyone, including the most random of people.

But not with Dave.

They met at a cool pub she wanted to check out. They'd agreed to just meet for a drink, so she ate before. (This will become relevant soon.)

She met him inside, and he was cute, smelled good and was dressed well, so she was excited to see where things might go.

She told him a little about herself and then asked some questions about him.

She was careful not to talk about herself the whole time—nobody likes that—but when she asked questions, he responded with one-word answers.

He then ordered food, much to Beth's disappointment, as she knew at this point that it was going to feel like a very long date if he couldn't pull up his socks and make some conversation.

She watched him eat his jambalaya while wishing she was at home watching a rom-com. He asked her nothing about herself, not one

65

thing, and continued to give minimal responses to her questions.

It got to the point where Beth ran out of ideas, so she improvised and started looking around at the art on the wall. One of the paintings was of a man playing the saxophone, and since she was running out of things to say, she randomly asked, "Do you like jazz music?"

Crickets.

After what seemed like enough time for him to go back through time and mentally list every band he'd ever heard, he mumbled a quiet yes.

An hour and a half into their date, she'd given it her all and she was done. But Dave escorted her outside and insisted on walking her home, the most he'd said all night.

Beth told him she was fine and would make it home on her own, and that's when he said it. "But we've barely talked all night."

She was flabbergasted. She'd pulled out all the stops to try and get this guy to open up a little, yet she got nothing! Just him chewing his food while she was reduced to pulling questions out of the decor.

She knew she couldn't sit through another date like that, so she texted him later to let him know she didn't feel the spark—and that was that.

LESSONS LEARNED

1. Always talk on the phone at least once before you meet on a date. If they can carry on a conversation over the phone, they should be able to do the same in person. It's a good test to see if your date is going to be filled with awkward silence.

2. Support local artists—they may just help you out on a date.

THE HOT MESS

While she was in nursing school, Jaya used to take the train back and forth into the city. One evening on her way home, a young man approached her and started chatting her up. Colin was really cute and funny, and there were scary old men staring at her, so she let him sit with her and they talked all the way to her stop.

He asked her if she'd like to grab a bite to eat and she agreed. They had a fun evening and at the end of the night, exchanged numbers.

They hung out a few more times, and after a week or two, he invited her to his place for dinner.

Jaya took the train downtown and managed to find his place. It was in a pretty sketchy area of town, and the building was old and run down. There were broken windows out front, boards missing from the side, and a homeless man sleeping near the entrance. Trying to ignore her feeling that this was no place for a woman alone, she texted him to hurry and let her in.

But the interior was not much better. When she stepped inside, she was hit hard by a rancid smell. It was so awful her involuntary first thought was, "This must be what death smells like!" She couldn't tell if it was rotten meat and old cigarettes, mould or some other disgusting combination of things she didn't even want to imagine.

The source of the stench became evident when she followed Colin into the kitchen. There were dirty dishes piled high in the sink, covered with flies. Half-eaten plates and containers of food were strewn across the counters. There were stains everywhere, from the floor to the ceiling.

Overhead, one dim lightbulb flickered, providing just enough light to reveal some kind of pink juice leaking out from the bottom of the fridge onto the floor. (She would later learn it was raw chicken juice ... gag.)

She didn't know what to say. She knew there was no way she'd be caught dead eating in a place like that; she'd probably end up with raging food poisoning and shit her pants on the way home.

There was drug paraphernalia on the coffee table and the carpet was filthy. Jaya badly needed to pee after the train ride, so she excused herself to the bathroom. Bad, bad idea. The bathroom made the kitchen look clean—there was pee and pubic hair all over the seat, and the smell of wet, mouldy towels almost caused her to upchuck.

She realized she couldn't even pee in this dump; she'd rather go outside in the bushes near the homeless man. She quickly grabbed her jacket and said she had to go.

Colin looked surprised and asked why she was leaving.

She just said, "Would you let your mom eat here?"

He didn't have much to say after that.

LESSONS LEARNED

1. If he lives in a sketchy neighbourhood but you trust him and want to see his place, meet in a coffee shop nearby and go together. If it doesn't feel safe, it probably isn't. Why take chances?

2. If a guy can't clean his place up when a woman comes over for dinner, he doesn't know how to treat and respect women. Move on.

THE BEAUTIFUL DRUNKEN FOOL

A few years back, Jayme met Sam on a dating site, and after a few days of texting, they decided to meet for dinner and drinks. On paper, he seemed to have it all: a job (that actually paid money), a house (that wasn't owned by his parents), a winning smile (with a full set of pearly whites) and a cute ass (no additional info needed here). Sam took a cab to the pub because he was nursing a broken ankle and sporting a set of crutches. Jayme thought it was cute that he still wanted to meet up despite his injury, so she offered to drive him home at the end of the night. He was really handsome and had gorgeous hair; even the crutches were somehow sexy on him.

The local hockey team was in the playoffs, and we Canadians love our hockey, so their plan was to sit front and centre to watch the game on TV.

Now, Jayme really wanted to impress him, so she kind of went to an extreme. She bought a team jersey the day before just so she would really fit in with the crowd. (Plus it looked totally cute on her.) But she was a playoff fan only, so she left the tag on it and strategically placed her hair and accessories so it wasn't visible; she'd be returning it the very next day. She felt guilty, but not too guilty—the jersey was almost three hundred bucks. She was sure it didn't cost more than $20 to make and the billionaire team owners would probably be okay without her support.

As the game went on, things were heating up on the screen, and so was the speed at which Sam was downing his drinks. He was also yelling at the television while pointing and cursing like a sailor. Each time the other team scored or got a penalty, he roared drunkenly at the TV and everyone around them stared.

> When Jayme told us this story, she said she actually wished she could crawl under the table and hide her head in her vagina at this point. Her next thought was that someone with their head up their vagina would be noticed quite quickly, of course, but we mention this just to emphasize how embarrassed she was.

While he continued to down double whiskeys with Coke, she delicately sipped on her wine.

After what seemed like an eternity, the game ended (the home team lost, it was tragic) and the bill came. At this point, Sam was so wasted he could hardly speak, let alone function on crutches. He could barely get his wallet out of his jeans, and Jayme sure as hell wasn't making a move to pay for the exorbitant amount of alcohol he drank in comparison to her single glass of wine. She kept her eyes on the floor, too embarrassed to make eye contact with the waitress who was watching Sam with a pitying expression on her face. He fumbled with the debit machine, attempting to punch in his pin numerous times, each time getting it wrong. It was painful.

This was the night that Jayme learned that, if you punch in your pin number wrong more than three times, you're SHUT OUT!

> *The moment of truth. Does she pay the $120 bill for this disastrous evening? Does she pretend she doesn't know this complete idiot and walk away? Well, you guessed it. She paid. She didn't want the waitress to have to pay for his complete and utter incompetence.*

It probably doesn't have to be said that Jayme was regretting her promise to drive him home, especially when she had to help him to the car. She asked him for directions to his place, and they ended up driving around in circles because he couldn't get his shit together and figure out where he lived. At one point he fell asleep, and she had to reach over and shake him awake.

They finally found his place, and he fumbled with his crutches while trying to get the car door open. At one point a crutch hit the window so hard she thought it would shatter the glass, and he barely missed her eye socket with another wild swing.

She never spoke to Sam again, even to collect his share of the ridiculous liquor bill. She was able to return the jersey but vowed never to mess with consumer karma again.

LESSONS LEARNED

1. If a guy orders a second double on your first date, discreetly signal your server, pay for your drink and dart. It's going to go downhill fast from here.

2. When someone on crutches orders a double whisky, ask him how much he weighs, because you may be carrying him out. If it isn't in your lift zone, it's time to go.

3. Never do anything in preparation for a date that you'll feel bad about if that date goes way, way wrong. If you wouldn't buy that jersey for a meetup with your girlfriends, do not do it for a potential Mr. Right. The odds are just too low.

IT'S NOT THE MOST WONDERFUL TIME OF THE YEAR ...

It's always nice to meet someone around the holidays. Everything is festive, romantic and cozy. That's why, when Tegan met Logan at a friend's Christmas party, she got that warm fuzzy feeling inside. She was excited to get out and meet some new people, and when she connected with Logan, it really felt like things were going her way! He was tall (a non-negotiable prerequisite for her), pretty good looking, and he seemed nice.

But after they'd chatted for a while, he went to refill his drink and started talking to another girl. Tegan was disappointed and slightly pissed—she definitely won't beg for attention. Her policy is that if a guy wants her, he has to work for it.

Shaking it off, she left the room and talked to other people. As she was leaving the party later, though, Logan approached her and said he'd like to get to know her better.

See, she knew he was interested! She told him he could find her on social media. (It was her way of playing a little hard to get, instead of just throwing her number at him.)

He started following her and the next day he sent her a message. She was pleased to hear from him, and they planned a date for a couple of weeks down the road.

They met at a restaurant for appetizers and drinks, and he looked good. But the conversation was a little boring. A few times she even noticed his eyes drifting to the television screen behind her head so he could check out the hockey game. Bad move. (Although she admits that if some kind of celebrity news were on, she'd probably do the same thing.) She realized that she wasn't feeling "it," and she usually gets it right away when she's into a guy. You know: butterflies, tingly feelings or that feeling where you want to shove your boobs in their face, hard.

But, for some reason, when they left the restaurant and he asked if she wanted to join him for some wine at his place, she said yes.

We know the reason–wine. Wine is the reason.

Perhaps she'd feel more of a spark in a different environment, she thought. Or maybe it just seemed like a good idea to go somewhere warm because it was snowing and freezing and she had her favourite, not-at-all-waterproof boots on. The transit system had stopped running, and she also knew a cab would be a solid hit to the bank account. But let's not get into those mundane details ...

They got to his house and Tegan asked if she could charge her phone; the battery was about to die. She always liked to know it wasn't going to let her down while she was on a date; ya just never know what might happen!

They sat on the couch, and he poured some wine before putting on music and sliding closer. She knew he wanted to make a move, but she did NOT want to reciprocate. She awkwardly twisted her body a bit, so her back was kind of to him, hoping that would give him the "definitely not" signal.

He picked up on it and got up to use the washroom. As he passed Tegan's phone on the counter, he unplugged it and tossed it onto the couch beside her, saying, "Here, you can text all your boyfriends now."

What the fuck!? She'd barely been on her phone all evening, except for a text here and there to her friend to let her know how the date was going. He came back from the bathroom and had the audacity to ask who she was texting. She couldn't believe he was acting jealous already! Well, hey, better to know now than later.

She looked at him and replied, "You're not my boyfriend. I don't owe you any type of answer to that question."

She could see him visibly struggling to change his attitude, but the shift in his tone was so dramatic it caught her off-guard.

"Listen—I'm attracted to you, you're attracted to me. I think we should have sex," he said.

At that point, Tegan says she remembers thinking she might puke in her mouth a bit. (She couldn't hide the disgusted look on her face even while she was telling us this story.)

She said, "Why? Because I went on a date with you, we should have sex? Why would that be expected of me?"

He didn't seem impressed at all. His only response was to get up and head into his bedroom.

Tegan knew she should just sleep on the couch, but it was hard leather with no cushions or pillows and she was really tired. After weighing her options, she followed him and found him already down to his boxers. He'd lit a candle beside the bed.

She lay down as far away from him as possible, fully clothed.

He turned to her and said, "So, are we going to do anything or what?"

She turned to face the wall and responded with a simple "no."

His response?

"Can you blow out the candle then?"

That was the end of that.

Tegan fell asleep until her alarm woke her a few hours later. Thank goodness she'd remembered to set it! She was terrified of waking him and having to deal with more questions or attitude, so she snuck out of bed, grabbed her shit and left. She felt like she was in a movie; she didn't even put her boots on until she was in the elevator. She tried not to fall over while jumping up and down trying to get them on and then struggled into her jacket. Outside, she was greeted with even more snow than the night before, so she called a cab. (She couldn't walk anywhere in those damn boots. Ugh—the things we do for beauty!)

Tegan didn't hear from Logan, and she wasn't terribly disappointed.

Then, out of the blue one day a few weeks later, he texted her to say he was surprised he hadn't heard from her. (Um, was this guy nuts?? Why on earth would she want to see him again?!) He invited her to a party with some friends that evening, but she declined and even called him out on his behaviour the last time they were together.

That's when he told her he somehow didn't remember a thing from that night. He made her tell him the story over and over again. She couldn't really tell if he was sincere, but he did apologize. She accepted his apology and moved on, thankful she dodged that bullet.

LESSONS LEARNED

1. If a guy is paying more attention to a hockey game than you on a date, he's probably not worth your time. (Unless he bought you tickets to a game, 'cause that's just cool.)

2. Jealous comment on a first date? So not cool. See it for the huge red flag it is and maybe tell him you're sexting your ex-boyfriend—just for kicks.

3. If he can't remember how he behaved on your date, give him a friendly reminder, but consider adding some juicy details, like "we had a threesome, but you couldn't get it up."

THE HOT
SWEATY MESS

Jasmine met Chad for the first time on a hot summer day. His online dating profile said he was a 5'11", hardworking and funny guy. He seemed to have his shit together.

They met in a parking lot near his home, and she had her usual nervous jitters, but she felt like this one was going to be different. (Note: this was not the first time she'd felt this, nor would it be the last.)

As soon as she saw him walking toward the car, she wanted to run away. He was about four inches shorter than his profile said he was and was dressed like a high school kid who had just come from the skate park.

Jasmine had taken the time to pick out a dress, do her hair and apply make-up, and here he was looking like he'd just rolled out of bed and thrown on the first items of clothing he saw.

She thought about faking a heavy period flow as an excuse to cut things short. But, since she is a big sucker, she put on a brave face and went ahead.

> *Side note:* We just don't understand why some guys come across as somebody completely different on their profile than they are in real life.

> We're going to figure it out when we meet you, and then we'll
> know you're:
>
> a. not the height (or age or whatever) you said you were;
> b. insecure about yourself, which is not an attractive
>   quality; and
> c. a big liar. A big untrustworthy lying liar.

They walked to a nearby restaurant. Now, we mentioned that it was a hot day, right? By the time they arrived, Chad was drenched in sweat and so red in the face that Jasmine thought she might need to perform CPR on him. (And it isn't easy to perform lifesaving measures in a dress.)

They sat on the patio, even though Jasmine suggested they sit inside where it was cooler, and ordered a drink. The conversation was so painful she thought about inserting the fork from the little cutlery bin into her left eye just so she'd know she was still alive.

Finally, the bill came. (He paid, for which she was very appreciative.) Then Chad suggested they go up to his place for a drink. At that moment, Jasmine wanted nothing more in the whole world than to run to her car, climb in, blast the air conditioning and get the hell out of there. She very politely said she was going to head home, but he continued to urge her to come up to his place; she continued to decline.

He then started coming up with alternative reasons for her to go up to his place.

> One of our favourites is when he explained he had had a
> piece of metal stuck in his hand and had kept it as a "prize"
> after having it removed—and he wanted her to see it.

This guy just would not get the message.

"NO, I DO NOT WANT TO GO TO YOUR PLACE!" Jasmine said to herself, politely squelching the urge to scream it out loud.

They finally got to her car. She thanked him again for the drink and climbed in. Just when she thought he had walked away, her car door opened. Chad reached in and rolled her window down before closing the door again—so he could continue talking to her.

Her car was running, and she was getting more and more antsy. She didn't want to talk to this guy anymore, and it was just becoming more awkward. She put the car into reverse, but he continued to speak to her through the window.

"Let's go on a hike!"

"What kind of car is this?"

Blah blah blah.

"Shoot me now," she thought. ("But bury me in this dress 'cause this shit is hot and cost me a fortune.")

Eventually, she hit her maximum patience limit and started backing out of the spot, assuming he'd get the message and back away from the car.

It was then that he started walking beside the car, still talking. Jasmine slowly sped up, and he started to jog, still holding onto the car door, still talking. It occurred to her that this was not safe, and she tried to guess how much she would need for bail money should she get arrested for accidentally running him over.

He finally let go, and she was finally free.

> Guys, we'll keep saying it until you hear it: no means no. Walking away means no. Not returning your texts or calls means no. Driving away means no. And–lest that not be clear enough–fuck no.

LESSONS LEARNED

1. Unless they are actually over 6'4", most guys are at least one inch shorter than stated in their profile. True fact. (If they are over 6'4", it's possible they are at least one inch taller than stated in their profile.)

   For the guys: lying about one inch is stretching the truth. Two inches or more is "there is no way to come back from this." We're not blind, and you're not honest.

2. If a guy is sweating after walking one block, you better like sweat, because ... well, visualize what he'll look like above you during sex.

MR. KNOWS
WHAT HE WANTS

Have you ever had a connection with a guy on an online dating site that seems so perfect you're almost scared to meet? One where the emails are so funny and witty, grammatically correct and sweet that you think, "This is the one!"?

Caitlyn has too, and his name was Jimmy.

They'd been chatting via email for a week or so, and he was hilarious. She loved his sense of humour right off the bat, and on paper, he seemed completely normal and down to earth.

They decided to meet at a restaurant, and as soon as he walked in, her heart skipped a beat. He had good hair, great style and an ass you could crack a walnut on.

They managed to get a seat on the busy patio. It was bustling with people and laughter, and Caitlyn was loving the vibe. She ordered a fruity martini, he ordered a beer, and they got down to chatting. That's when it happened—he started talking about himself, and the cockiness spilt out all over the table.

He started off by saying, "I don't know why I'm fucking single.

"I'm fucking confident. I've got a fucking job."

Wow, well okay then, what more could a gal want?!

Caitlyn decided she was going to need a double martini instead of just a classy single. Then she decided to delve into his singleness a little more. She asked him what he looked for in a woman, and his response was, "Well, I like tits. And nice arms."

Off to a good start.

So, Caitlyn summarized, she was eating dinner with a guy who was basically looking for anyone with tits and arms. Narrowing it down to 51% of the world's population, more if you include man-boobs.

He proceeded to tell her how he believed in the paranormal, and how he was going to get a "fucking video camera" and his friend's "fucking dog," and stay overnight in a "fucking haunted house" "'cause dogs can sense shit."

It wasn't long before Caitlyn had chewed her nails down to the point of drawing blood. She had ordered a third double martini she didn't really want, and she was missing *Grey's Anatomy*. (This was back in the McSteamy days, so she wasn't happy.) She was also completely humiliated; she was sure the people nearby on the crowded patio couldn't help overhearing his constant profanity and must think he was off his rocker.

She wasn't sure which was more painful, her disappointment about how Jimmy "the one" had turned out to be Jimmy "would it really be unforgivable to go to the bathroom and not come back?" or her embarrassment.

He continued spewing out stories: he could, for example, play drums and guitar at the same time while being suspended by a pulley system in his basement. (A for creativity; F for mental images that wouldn't be considered sexy in any universe.)

The bill finally came. He then told her (to the cent) what she owed for dinner, and asked her out again, confirming her suspicion he hadn't noticed she hadn't said 10 words in the previous hour and felt like she might cry.

What she wanted to say was, "I'd rather get kicked in the face by a donkey and lose all my teeth than spend another moment at this table with you." But—karma. She took the high road and said, "I don't think we're a match." Then she went to the bathroom to call a cab to drive her drunk ass home!

LESSONS LEARNED

1. When breasts and/or any other body part are in the top two of a guy's romance wish list, resist your urge to throat punch him and just back away slowly.

2. If asked what your thoughts are on the paranormal, roll your eyes into the back of your head, blink quickly, start to drool and pee your pants. You may win an Academy Award, depending on who is in the restaurant. Your date will finish early—and he might even pick up the bill, given your paranormal powers.

3. If you believe that someone can play drums and guitar at the same time while suspended from a pulley system in the ceiling, we applaud your imagination, but we need to talk.

DAMNED IF YOU DO

Jess was set up with Barney by a mutual friend. Now, this always seems like a good idea at first—he must be a decent guy if he's a friend of a friend, right?

But it could go either way. She could really like him, or he could be a total knob that gives her a rash and then she's stuck in an awkward position when their mutual friend asks how it went. That said, her friends knew the dating struggle was real, so they were willing to take the risk.

Okay, here's how it went. They chatted for a couple of days before deciding to meet. He was really outgoing, had a great career, was in the process of buying his own home and was extremely polite.

On the day in question, he picked her up and they headed out for brunch. He was cute, with a fabulous smile and a terrific sense of humour. As they enjoyed their eggs benny, the topic of religion came up. Now Jess is not, and has never been, religious. But that doesn't mean she doesn't accept other people's beliefs, and she was totally open to discussing it. She was also open to dating a guy on a different spiritual path, even though she had tried it in the past and found it tough. He asked her if she was a Christian. She said she wasn't, but that she was a spiritual person.

It turned out that not only was he a Christian, but his mom was a pastor. He attended church every Sunday and Bible study every Wednesday. Oh, and he didn't drink alcohol or swear. Ever.

So not only did Jess' vision of a filthy sexual encounter full of hot dirty words fly out the window, but the drinks they were going to have to get them to that point did as well. That would leave her with the option of sober sex, using a clean vocabulary that might include such encouraging phrases as "darn, that feels nice," or "yes, do put that there, please," and perhaps, "oopsie; in the poopsie."

But she really enjoyed his company, and he seemed to enjoy hers, so after they finished brunch, they decided to do some home decor shopping for his new place. She had to admit he was a ton of fun to hang out with, and she could see why their friends thought they'd get along.

Six hours later they decided to have tea at his house and watch some TV. To her surprise, Jess felt a hand creep across the couch and then slide its way between her legs. Now surely it couldn't be his hand, not after he'd been so clear and upfront about his devout Christianity.

> *Perhaps it was her hand—sometimes us gals just reach for our vaginas at random times, don't we? No? It's just us?*

The next thing she knew, Jess and Barney were in the throes of a passionate make-out session. When clothes started coming off, though, she pulled away and said, "Wait—isn't this against your belief system?"

Barney's response was that he sometimes made decisions that he knew God wouldn't agree with. Errrr, okay. That being clarified, they moved on to some hot sex.

But partway through, Barney suddenly stopped. He said he couldn't "release" himself or he'd feel "conviction." (Which apparently is a religious term that means something like "alerted to our sins by God"—does not sound good.)

Okay, what the hell?!

He politely offered her a baby wipe.

The whole situation was odd—and then Jess started feeling like she was being judged by the almighty!

Jess left feeling a wee bit of shame (which passed after a few martinis and a slew of curse words she reeled off in front of her girlfriends).

Barney messaged her a few days later, asking if she wanted to hook up again. Really???

She took it as a compliment but passed. She decided to stick with guys who can get tipsy and swear from time to time. After all, they might need liquid courage to keep up with her!

LESSONS LEARNED

1. Guys who shop for home decor on the first date want sex—it's a ploy!

2. Tea may also lead to sex when you least expect it. (Apparently.)

BURNED BY ALADDIN'S LAMP

Cate met Ali through one of those swipe dating apps. She'd hit a real low—she even swiped right on him when he had no bio write-up and didn't include his height. It was strictly based on his photos: he had a dazzling smile and great hair.

They messaged back and forth and actually hit it off. He seemed down to earth and gentlemanly (and by that, Cate means he didn't write anything about his junk or suggest banging her within the first few messages).

They decided to meet for a drink, a harmless glass of wine. She parked near his place, and he came downstairs to meet her at the door.

Now Ali has smoking dark eyes and mocha skin. He smelled like one of those aftershave samples you get in a magazine, the kind you want to take to bed with you and rub all over your pillows.

They walked to a nearby pub and ordered wine. One glass turned into three, and at one point Cate felt like they were the only two people in the world. The conversation was so deep and intense, like nothing she'd ever experienced before. They talked about their childhoods, their dreams, their goals and just life in general.

She couldn't stop gazing into his deep dark eyes. She'd never met a guy like this; it was like he had some kind of hold on her. (No—we see where you're heading, but she had not been roofied.)

It was decided that she was too tipsy to drive, so they went back to his place so she could sober up and they could chat some more.

Somehow, though, she ended up with a gin and tonic in hand, cuddled up on his couch with R&B playing in the background. The lights were low.

They always get ya with the soft lighting!

At this point, Cate would like to note that she had smoked marijuana less than five times in her life, so no, she's not an addict, but yes, she gave into peer pressure. She hadn't smoked at all in almost 20 years, mostly because the last time made her throw up her tortellini in the neighbourhood grocery store. But when Ali offered her some, his suave ways and caramel-chocolate eyes made her think that it was time for her to break out of her 36-year-old shell and give it another whirl.

They drank and smoked, and the next thing she knew she was naked in his living room. (A few hours later she would realize he had no curtains, and there was a lovely condo building right next door full of people with a perfectly clear view.)

They ended up having sex, and it turned into something out of an erotic book. At one point, she looked up from the bed to find him standing beside her, completely naked and smoking weed, his erection so dangerously close to her face she had to stop herself from playfully swatting it away.

Next, he explained that he wanted to role play. He wanted her to pretend she was married and say she was going to go home to tell her husband she just had dirty sex with another man. She looked around for cameras—this HAD to be one of those situations where she was being filmed; this shit was just getting too crazy! He even used the term "raw dog" as a way of letting her know he wanted to remove his condom. (Since she's a safety girl, the answer was no.)

Then, out of nowhere, an overwhelming feeling of dry mouth hit her. She felt like she'd eaten a jar of sand and realized it must have been the weed. She slid off him (she was on top at this point) and ran to the kitchen for water. That's when nausea hit, and she ran into his bathroom, projectile vomiting into his toilet.

When she finally stopped heaving, she decided she might in fact be dying and needed to leave right then and there. She grabbed her stuff and left him standing naked in his kitchen (with blue balls, we're assuming), the smell of fresh vomit wafting out of the bathroom.

Cate somehow managed to make it to her friend's house for the night. Thankfully it was one of those friends who always has an extra tooth-brush and who will tie your hair back while you retch your guts out.

She didn't think for a moment that she'd hear from him again—but the next day, he let her know he was ready for round two!!! It just goes to show you, girls: even if you aren't a porn star and you leave your stomach contents in their bathroom, guys will STILL want to have sex with you! Yay us!!!

She didn't take him up on his offer. She sees herself as more of a lover, not a cheater.

LESSONS
LEARNED

1. Don't do drugs. If you do drugs, do them with people you know and trust and who will hold your hair back while you puke.

2. Watch for mood lighting: if he doesn't have photosensitivity, it means he wants sex ASAP.

3. Check for curtains before you get naked in the living room unless you're down with that kinda thing.

4. The only time a guy should say "raw" and "dog" in the same sentence is when he's buying you a hot dog with onions. (The all-beef kind, not the cheap kind.)

THE FILTHY, FILTHY REALTOR

Julia met Bob on a free online dating site.

> *We often wonder if the free sites are worse than the paid ones, but we've had shit luck on both.*

Anyway, when the time came, Bob and Julia met at a restaurant, and he was a babe. (Do people use that term nowadays?) He was tall, blond and in fantastic shape. He had teeth that could have been on a poster in the dentist's office. He worked as a realtor and was super easy to talk to.

They had a couple of drinks and shared an appetizer, laughing and sharing stories. Then he paid the bill—with zero awkwardness. Things were going swimmingly! He did at one point answer a phone call, and it was his mother, which made things slightly awkward. But overall the date was decent. Quite decent, in fact.

They walked out to the parking lot and hugged goodbye, and then somehow his tongue was in her mouth. The kiss was fine, a little intense, but then he pulled back and said, "Let's go back to your house and have sex."

Um, okay, slow down there, dude. Julia was a lady!

> *Sure. We say that about ourselves too!*

She told him she wasn't interested in having a one-night stand and decided to call it a night. As much as she would have liked to see him naked, she went with her gut and passed. He seemed like the kind of guy who would hit it and quit it, and she wasn't down for that.

As she got into her car, he came up behind her, placed his hands on her hips, and whispered: "I wanna bend you over the backseat of your car."

Okay wow, but no. Also, she probably had an empty McDonald's bag in there that she didn't want him to see—he definitely didn't look like the McDonald's type ... that body. Okay, we gotta move on here.

So off she went, homeward bound. She got home and received a text message from him. She expected the usual; something along the lines of "I had a great time," "Can I see you again?" or "You look like a Disney princess, and your body should be in a Victoria's Secret catalogue." You know.

But alas, Bob's text read, "Send me a picture of you dripping wet."

Okay, seriously??? They shared an appetizer, not a steak dinner with a $200 bottle of wine on a private plane on their way to see a Broadway show. (You might get a picture after that, just saying.)

Julia was shocked and completely turned off. She told him she wasn't interested and wished him well.

A few days later, he texted her to ask what she was up to, and she responded with a random, just-being-polite answer—"I'm working" or something along those lines. He then proceeded to ask her if she was "flicking" her "bean" and thinking of him.

> *Okay, who even says "flicking the bean?"*

So what did Julia do in this situation? Well, just what any other girl would do (or should do). She googled "vagina images," cropped one that looked terrifying and hideous, and sent it to him with an "I don't think we're a good match" message.

Thankfully, that was the end of filthy Bob.

LESSONS LEARNED

1. Be wary of people that have funny pet names for masturbating.

2. If a guy asks for a dirty picture after the first date, he's not boyfriend material. And if you're ever tempted, remember how easy it would be for him to show the guys at work, the guys at the gym, the guys at the game—and so on.

MOMMY & DADDY ISSUES

Matt and Vanessa met online two years ago during the summer and hit it off. He was super cute, funny, charismatic, and always kept up with his side of the texting and phone calls. They met for coffee for their first date; he loved Disneyland, kids, hiking and lots of other things that sparked her interest.

He did disclose that he came from a broken home, had a strained relationship with his father, and had issues with commitment. Well okay, no problem, they were just having coffee here so no need to divulge everything. (Perhaps Vanessa came across as a therapist type. She'd had many guys pour their hearts out to her on first dates and then never heard from them again.)

They decided to get together a second time, and the next date, they played pool and had drinks. It was fun, but there was something odd that Vanessa just couldn't put her finger on. Call it a woman's intuition or a sixth sense, but it rubbed her the wrong way. Anyway, she tried to ignore the feeling and enjoy the date.

When he got home that night, he texted to ask if she'd like to meet him and his friends at the casino. Normally she wouldn't mind, but something was telling her to take her time with this guy. She told him she wouldn't be able to make it.

The next day, he told Vanessa his mom was coming into town for the long weekend and asked if she'd like to hang out with them. (Remember, this would have been their third date.)

She thought to herself, "Slow down there, cowboy, I don't even know your last name!"

She asked him if he didn't feel like that was moving ahead a bit too quickly, and he didn't seem to think it was a big deal—he just said his mom was "cool and easy to get along with."

She dodged meeting Mom.

Vanessa's instinct was to run, but because she was looking for a relationship somewhat desperately, she continued to hang out with him and they talked on a regular basis.

That said, he hadn't even kissed her yet.

After their fourth date, Vanessa decided to call and ask him how he was feeling about their dates so far. Apparently, it pushed some kind of button, because he responded by defensively asking her why she wanted to move so quickly.

She was so confused!!!

She told him that she was the one who wanted to take things slow, and he was the one who wanted her to meet his friends and his mother within the first week. She thought he might have a philosophical or at least interesting response, but no.

Instead, he said, "My condo is on fire, I gotta go," and hung up the phone.

She was worried about him and happened to be out and nearby, so she drove by his building. There was no smoke or fire trucks in sight.

Vanessa never heard from Matt again. But a couple of days later his profile was back online with a new shiny photo. She asked herself how she always found the emotionally unavailable guys with commitment issues—or if there is just a very high percentage of emotionally unavailable guys with commitment issues?

LESSONS LEARNED

1. If a guy asks you to meet his mother after two dates, tap out. Something peculiar is going on there.

2. If he talks about his daddy issues on the first date, take it as a red flag. First date convo should be light and fluffy, like rainbows and kittens and favourite sexual positions.

3. If you haven't received a kiss by date four, he:

   a. Is gay and just really likes you;
   b. Has commitment issues—and you need to back away; or
   c. Is recovering from a case of cold sores. Just be thankful.

THE DANCING FOOL

We think it's likely you'll ask yourself, "Why the hell did she stay with this guy?" as you read this story. Well, Tanya asked herself that many times.

She met Brady in a dive bar in the city and there were warning signs right away. But did she pay attention? Hell no! She fell for his smooth dance moves, dark eyes and mysterious swagger. He casually started dancing with her, then grinding up on her. No "hey" or "hi," just some smooth moves. He smelled like stale cigarettes, which was normally a turn off for Tanya, but apparently not on this night.

She made eye contact with her friend who was giving her the "hell no!!" look, but did she listen? Hell no! Later, she invited him back to her place, and as they walked to the cab, she noticed he was dripping with gold jewelry like a rapper.

He didn't utter a single word on the cab ride to her house; he barely spoke until they sat down in her living room. In fact, the first full sentence out of his mouth was when he pulled out some drugs and asked if she wanted a "bump."

Despite a hundred red flags waving, they hooked up.

Tanya noticed that, unlike other guys she'd been with, he didn't, um, go down on her. She thought maybe it was because he was drunk and high, or maybe because she was all sweaty, so she just forgot about it. In the morning, she waited for him to leave and had already decided she was fine with not seeing him again. She figured he'd just leave without saying anything, but he casually asked for her number, and somehow, again, she agreed.

A couple of weeks later, after some sporadic texting, they hooked up again. And again he didn't, um, go down on her. She was beginning to think she had a vaginal problem that he was picking up on. Or maybe he didn't know how to do it? Maybe he was nervous? Maybe she needed to force his head down there? She finally decided to call him out on it; I mean, what's fair is fair! He should return the favour.

He told her that he only did it to girls he was exclusive with.

Wow, even we've never heard that excuse before, and we wrote the book on bad dates!

Okay. Perhaps she'd abstain from doing any kind of oral activity on him if that's how he was going to be! On the third or fourth hook up, he finally went in for the kill, and it was kinda basic, but she was just happy it happened. She was actually starting to warm up to this guy. He had a pretty decent sense of humour and was easy to talk to—it just took him a while to break out of his shell.

After a few weeks, Tanya and Brady had the "exclusive" discussion. She was happy seeing other people but still hooking up with him from time to time. He wanted them to be exclusive—but only for sex. After a summer of crazy hookups and unpredictable nights out, she realized she was okay with having an exclusive situation for a while.

It remained that way for a few weeks. They got together a couple of times a week and Tanya was happy with that.

Fast forward about a month, and she realized she was just plain bored with Brady. They never really went anywhere, just hung around her place. He wasn't the best conversationalist, and if she was going to dedicate herself to sex with only one person, that person better be worth it!

She wanted to start seeing other people, since she was ready for something a little more serious. She decided it was time to let Brady know how she was feeling. She ended things, and he seemed to take it well. They decided they'd keep in touch and remain friends.

A few days after their break-up (if you can call it that), he posted a photo on one of his social media accounts. Tanya decided to creep the comments and noticed that some hot girl had posted a kiss emoji. It seemed odd since he'd been "non-exclusive" for just a few days, so she decided to delve into the situation a little more. She checked out the girl's profile, and lo and behold, there was a photo of her, scantily clad, in a seductive pose with a guy's arm draped over her body. And to whom did this arm belong? The distinctive sleeve tattoo gave it away; it was the one that Tanya had been oh so attracted to when she saw him that first night.

The date of the photo you ask? Well, it was well within the time-frame of Tanya and Brady's "exclusivity" situation. Interesting! So "exclusive" meant it was okay for him to be with other girls, but not for Tanya to be with other guys? Sleazeball! Thanks to the advanced features of smartphones, she screenshot the photo and sent it to him with a sweet message that said something like "go" and "fuck" and "yourself." She blocked him on every single source of communication she could think of and they never spoke again.

LESSONS
LEARNED

1. Just too many to list here. We'll let Tanya's sad story lay down the learning, like an electric tattoo on the brain.

2. Okay, just one: if a guy acts like a sleazeball, talks like a sleazeball and looks like a sleazeball, chances are very good HE IS A SLEAZE-BALL. No, let us rephrase that more clearly: HE IS A FUCKING SLEAZEBALL.

WHEN SHIT GETS REAL

Madeline had known Michael for a few years. They'd worked together at a club, and she felt like she knew him pretty well. She was attracted to him and his wild personality.

Now, he could be a bit too much at times. Madeline also knew he had a bit of a temper on him—but a lot of us do, right?? They started hanging out a lot when Madeline broke up with her boyfriend. She wanted to see if it could become something. (He had also just broken up with his girlfriend.)

Madeline occasionally gets free tickets from work and had tickets to a Mariners game in Seattle. She knew Michael loved Seattle, so she invited him. He booked a hotel and planned out a night.

But Madeline could feel Michael was somehow different than when they were friends. His mental state seemed off. He was buying things all the time and spending insane amounts of money—cameras, trucks and thousands on clothes. He kept talking about how powerful and rich they were going to be, except he didn't have a job and wasn't really looking for one.

As the weekend approached, she was so concerned with his behaviour that she thought of ending it with him altogether. But she told herself the trip would let her know for sure either way.

During the drive to the States, there was a strange vibe. His behaviour was still off, and they didn't stop fighting for the entire drive.

When they got to the game, she started feeling sick, so when he asked her what she wanted to eat or drink, she said, "Just water." (He'd been drinking since they arrived in Seattle.) After 15 minutes, he came back with two hot dogs, two pretzels, a big bucket of popcorn, crackerjacks, peanuts and two beers. Ummm, what??? When she asked for her water (pointing out that she wouldn't be able to touch any of the food because she felt so sick), he ran back to get it. After another 15 minutes, he came back. He had two more beers and no water. By this point Madeline was getting pissed, and he could tell, so he ran up again.

Two minutes later, a man she didn't know came down the stairs, pointed at Madeline and said to the security guard, "The guy that's with her tried to start a fight with me."

While most people would ask the guy what the hell he was talking about, she knew immediately. "Fuck!" she thought, as she grabbed her purse and headed up the stairs. At the top of the stairs, Michael was with the other security guards talking about how the guy started a fight with HIM. He was giving the guy evil looks from afar and at one point in the discussion, he actually said, "I'm a scout for the New York Yankees, and I cannot believe we are being treated like this."

Nope!! That was Madeline's breaking point. She said, "We are done here, let's go!" and stormed away. As they walked outside, she started in on him about his horrible and embarrassing behaviour. She was SO pissed off. When they (finally!) got outside of the stadium, she was still on a rant.

He did what any normal human being would do—he took off! Literally ran away from her at top speed. She can still remember his stupid little shaved head weaving through the crowd and then disappearing. She stood there, not really knowing where she was and not knowing what to do. Luckily, she had a room key with the name of the hotel on it, so she hailed a cab.

And there ends her horrible date in Seattle.

Just kidding!! It got WORSE!

Once she got back to the hotel, Michael kept calling her relentlessly, asking her to please meet him at the restaurant he said he had paid to make reservations at.

In hindsight, everything that had come out of his mouth that night and over the past few weeks was BS, and she should have stayed at the hotel. She would have saved herself so much embarrassment and hurt—but then we wouldn't be telling you this EPIC story.

She arrived at the restaurant first and was still a little frazzled as she grabbed a seat in a little corner booth. The waiter saw her miserable face and told her to cheer up as she ordered her favourite glass of wine. If he only knew! As she sipped, Michael came in the restaurant with a face that showed absolutely no remorse for what he had done. It didn't look like he was going to try to turn the night around.

As you can imagine, they ended up arguing at the table. Madeline was looking at the salmon on the menu, thinking about how hungry she was and how delicious it would be, if only she was at that restaurant with someone she liked.

She can't remember exactly what was said in the end. She's pretty sure she told him she'd never go on a date with him again let alone travel to another country with him.

Then she realized that the salmon wasn't going to be enjoyable at all; in truth, she realized she didn't want to sit there one moment longer. She pushed the menu back onto the table and said, "You know what? I'm leaving."

He responded with the last thing she expected. He said, "You know what? No. I'm going to leave!!" He stood up and reached for his full water glass.

In that second, she knew exactly what he was going to do.

He had once told her about an incident that happened a couple years before at a restaurant in Palm Springs with his then-girlfriend. The service, he said, was horrible, and as they left, he threw two wine glasses to the floor, smashing them.

So when Madeline saw him reach for the water glass, she knew there were going to be problems.

She looked up at him from her seat and with a shaky voice, asked, "What are you doing???" But she knew exactly what he was doing. He chucked the full water glass at the wall right beside her head.

As the broken glass and water hit her left arm, she remembers looking over at a table of young girls sitting with their mom. The last thing she wanted any little girl to see was a man treating a woman like this. But what exactly could she do in that moment?

She kept repeating "What are you doing? Stop it!!" He didn't stop there, oh no. He took his empty wine glass and chucked that at the wall. The stem broke off, and the glass flew back at him, so he chucked it again. By this time, everyone in that part of the restaurant was staring at them (obviously).

He turned around and ran out.

Lisa stared down at the seat and then at her arm, both covered with water and broken glass.

She felt terrible that the staff would have to deal with the mess and wondered if she should clean it up. She then realized that, despite the fact that all eyes in the restaurant were on her, not a single person had come over to see if she was okay. The people right beside her didn't utter a word. As she was about to look over at them and say, "I'm okay, thank you!" in her most sarcastic tone, the waiter who had previously told her to "cheer up" came over and said, "Baby, are you okay?"

She burst into tears. She was so shocked, hurt, angry and embarrassed. The waiter stood her up and helped her turn so that her back was to the restaurant. A manager came over and took over the situation like an absolute pro. He shone a flashlight up and down her arm to see if there was any glass that she didn't get off.

She kept apologizing. He said, "Honey, don't worry. We've seen it all here."

Madeline didn't know if that was true or not, but it didn't make her feel any better about the situation. He invited her over to the lounge so he could bring her another glass of wine on the house (in case any of the glass had flown into her wine—now that would have really pissed her off!) but she was paralyzed.

Finally, she said, "I can't turn around and face the people in this restaurant!" He was very persuasive. He put his arm around her, turned her around and led her to the lounge. People were still staring, and some men had stood up, in fight mode, trying to seem tough.

She thought, "Where were you guys five minutes ago when I actually needed you??"

Madeline sat in the lounge barely able to drink the wine they gave her. (She did end up downing it—it would have been rude not to!) She took out her phone and booked another room in the hotel she had planned to stay in with Michael. A different member of the staff came up to her every few minutes and offered to help. Another manager asked if she wanted them to call the police and one even came over with a box of tissues on the DL, so she wasn't so snotty and disgusting. (He didn't say that, but she assumed that's what he was thinking!)

A waitress even offered to drive her back to the hotel. Madeline was so impressed by the staff at this restaurant!

BTW, it was at the Met in downtown Seattle if you ever want to go. They were amazingly attentive and genuinely concerned for her. Madeline never had the chance to actually taste the food, but says it looked absolutely delicious. She's still looking forward to having the salmon when she's there next. :)

Madeline knew she had to make one last stop in the room Michael was staying in.

Why would she go back in the room, you ask? She was willing to leave without her make-up, clothes and camera, but she wouldn't get far without a passport. It's essential for a Canadian to have when leaving the USA, aka Trumpland. Our condolences, by the way.

She went upstairs to the room and used her key card to open the door. The door unlocked but as she pushed it, it opened only a crack. She realized that this absolute twat had bolted it. Of course! What else could go wrong?!! She yelled his name, banged on the door and called his cell phone. No response ... nada. At that moment, she had a mini mental breakdown. She sat on the ground and cried for about

10 seconds. It just needed to come out!

When that was over, she got up and marched downstairs. She asked the people at reception if they had a tool to unbolt the door. They did, but it was in a safe, they didn't know the code and the person who did wasn't answering the phone. How fucking convenient! Unlike the staff at the restaurant, the hotel staff were idiots. They came upstairs with her and tried yelling for Michael. No answer. They went downstairs and called him from the hotel line. Still nothing.

At that point, despite how shitty he'd made her feel that night, she started to get worried. What if he had done something really stupid? What if he could hear her yelling but couldn't respond? The last thing she wanted was for him to be hurt, so she got the hotel to call for help. Ten minutes or so later, two firefighters showed up and tried calling for him one more time. When there was no answer, they took an axe and crowbar and busted the door down.

Madeline stared in disbelief. She felt like she was in the fucking twilight zone. She could not believe that this is how the weekend had ended up! When the door busted open, they could see an empty bed. The doors to the kitchen and living room were closed. Madeline cowered behind the firefighters because she was terrified of what she was going to see. When they opened the doors, though, there he was on the pull-out couch, snoring away. Really!

The fire fighters woke him up and he looked confused and very scared. "Yes sir!" he said. Where were these manners a few hours before? She gathered her stuff quickly. Michael tried to talk her out of leaving. She ignored him, and the hotel employee walked her to her new room in complete silence. Not once did she ask what had happened or if Madeline was okay. It was horrible service.

Madeline got to her room, turned on the fireplace and just lay in bed wondering what the fuck had happened that night!

Many people, having heard the story thus far, ask Madeline, "How did you get home??"

Because, really, we'd love to end the story there. Well, initially, she booked a bus ticket back home. But the last thing she wanted to do after that weekend was spend five hours on a bus. Michael texted her and said she could get a ride back with him. She accepted. He owed her that much!

He was still an absolute prick on the way back, and when she brought up the situation, he started to speed up and drive dangerously.

Madeline dropped the topic and just focused on getting home.

Months later, Michael told Madeline that he had been diagnosed with bipolar disorder. She wasn't surprised, and hopes that he'll get the help he needs.

He also said he thinks they belong together and he loves her. Uh, nope. Not in this lifetime!! Madeline hasn't been to Seattle since, but when she does go, it will be with a stable man, and she'll be packing plastic cups. Just in case.

LESSONS LEARNED

1. We'd like to say something funny here, but mental illness just isn't something to laugh about. Neither is abuse, even if its worst outcome is humiliation and broken glass.

2. If you're dating someone whose behaviour puts him or you at risk in any way, first get yourself to safety. If the situation is serious enough to warrant it, call 911. Then—by phone or text—encourage him to get help. If you can reach his friends or family, let them know your concerns.

3. That is all. Unhealthy people can't have healthy relationships. It isn't possible. Save yourself.

NO DISTANCE TOO FAR

After her last break-up, Dion had decided she was never dating again. Fair enough: her ex-boyfriend had turned out to be a drug addict who ruined her credit by missing mortgage payments.

She lived the single life for about a year, randomly dating and hitting up clubs. She planned to find work overseas—to leave and never turn back. She felt like a fresh start was exactly what she needed. Convinced that good men didn't exist, she was looking forward to a life of solo travel.

One evening, at a club with friends, she noticed a guy standing at the bar, stirring his drink and glancing her way every now and then. He finally strolled over and sat beside her.

She could tell he was struggling to find something to say, and she could sense his nervousness. It apparently got the best of him because, without saying a word, he got up and strolled back to the bar to get another drink.

Dion figured he really wanted to talk to her, as he kept staring at her and walking past her seat now and then, but she continued to pay minimal attention to him until he came and sat down beside her again. This time, he managed to blurt out, "How's your night going?"

They talked, and he became more comfortable and chatty around her. She learned his name was Jessie. He bought her drinks and they ended up having a pretty decent conversation. There wasn't anything obviously special about him. Dion got hit on a lot and really thought nothing of it (except "yay" for free drinks). At the end of the night, when her friends were leaving, Jessie asked her to stay and hang out. He promised he'd drive her home, and she thought to herself, "Yeah, right. Um, no!" She left with her friends but gave him her number when he asked.

When he did call to ask her out, she already had plans but told him where she and friends were going. At the club, she hit the dance floor with her friends, and there he was, standing against the wall, watching her.

He asked if he could hang out with her and her friends, which was a bit awkward, but she agreed. He was persistent, and she kind of liked it. It ended up being a wonderful evening—so wonderful that Dion ended up at a hotel with Jessie for the night.

He kept appearing in her life over the following weeks, either showing up wherever she was or picking her up at the end of the night. That's when she realized she had a bit of a crush. She liked that he wasn't pushy, because she wasn't exactly sure how she felt, and she even ditched him at one point to hang out with another guy.

But for the next three months, he continued to find her in the clubs downtown, always making sure she had a drink in hand and a ride home.

It eventually occurred to her that she always casually mentioned where she'd be—maybe she was starting to like this guy!

One night when Dion was out with friends, Jessie showed up, but this time he had a group of girls around him, laying their hands on his arms and flirting.

Dion recognized she was jealous, and a part of her thought, "He's mine!"

She wanted to spend more time with him outside of the nightclub scene, and when she hinted at the idea, he let her know he wanted that too. For the next couple of months, they spent a lot of time together, and it seemed they were falling for each other.

But when summer was over and fall rolled around, Dion decided she still had the travel bug and wanted to see the world. She still expected very little from men in general and wanted to live her life.

She decided to move to Saudi Arabia to work for a year. She told Jessie he didn't need to wait for her but that she'd be happy to keep in touch while she was away, with no expectations.

They ended up talking every day, and she missed him immensely. She hadn't felt like this in a long time.

Jessie always made an effort to chat with her and even flew to Thailand to meet her for a quick getaway. She knew he was something special.

When the new year rolled around, Jessie told Dion that he worried she'd never come home and felt like his life was on hold.

She realized she needed to explore their relationship; she might miss out on something amazing if she stayed overseas much longer. She moved home, and their love story continued.

Two years later, they married—and they're now expecting their first child. After so many volatile, disappointing relationships, Dion really didn't think she'd ever feel this kind of love. It would have been easy for her to brush Jessie off and keep moving—but his persistence and her decision to come home ended up making their story ... a happy ever after.

LESSONS LEARNED

1. Travel, live, make mistakes—we need to in order to grow and learn about ourselves!

2. Open your heart for the guys who take time and make efforts for you. He may not be what you think you want initially, but over time, you may figure out he's exactly what you need.

BODILY FUNCTION MISHAPS

BEAUTY &
THE BEAST

Darla was a sizzling 20-something out on the town and ready for action. She frequented a particular hot spot every weekend with her sister, and they became friends with a group of people who went there almost every weekend too.

That's how she met Dean. She liked him almost immediately and found out through mutual friends that he liked her as well. After a few weekends of chatting at the bar, he invited her to a Halloween party. She decided that instead of dressing up in a typical scary costume (she obviously hasn't seen *Mean Girls*), she wanted to look pretty for him. She borrowed an absolutely fabulous princess dress and spent hours on her makeup.

He came to pick her up wearing an orange prison jumpsuit and didn't even compliment her amazing costume! Big mistake.

When they arrived at the party, she expected him to introduce her to his friends, but instead he found a seat in the corner of the room, told her to sit there and left her while he went to watch the hockey game. He didn't even make sure she had a drink or a snack, and she knew nobody.

Now Darla was admittedly a little insecure; she wasn't the type to strike out on her own and introduce herself to strangers. She felt so out of place that she was even too uncomfortable to get up to use the bathroom. She wanted to crawl under a rock and hide. After what felt like hours, he came over and said, "Okay, let's go."

"Let's go??"

She couldn't believe it.

With nothing else to do, she stood up and followed him to the car. A part of her was thankful to be away from the crowd of strangers, but the last thing she wanted to do was get in the car with him.

They made uncomfortable small talk on the way home. At her apartment, he walked her to the door of the building and said, "Do you want to swap spit?"

Now, as much as she'd liked him just a few hours before, this comment disgusted her BIG TIME and took the already revolting evening to a new low. She got up her nerve (the nerve she'd wished she'd had at the party) and told him no (never!).

The beautiful princess walked casually up the stairs to her building, keeping both glass slippers on her feet, never to look back! (Yes, we know we're mixing up fairy tales here.)

LESSONS LEARNED

1. Always carry cab fare and a charged mobile. If someone puts you in the corner without an excellent glass of wine and a charming someone to keep you company, split. No one puts Baby in the corner.

2. Someone that calls kissing "swapping spit" should be "slapped senseless." I mean, don't do it, that's assault—but really, a giant hand should just come out of the sky and WHACK!

GIRL'S GOTTA BREATHE

Jasmine and Nikki decided to check out one of the hottest patios in town. They went for a casual dinner with a few drinks, which turned into "dranks," if you know what we mean. It started classy and then got just plain messy (as some girls' nights do).

These girls ended up two drunken, foul-mouthed fools who should have been locked up in a padded room until they were sober.

This all happened on a Tuesday. Who gets like this on a Tuesday? Well, these girls did! They ended up at a local nightclub (we reiterate—it was Tuesday!) and it was—not surprisingly—almost completely empty.

Jasmine seemed to be slightly (okay, a lot) more drunk than Nikki, which was evidenced by the dance moves she was performing, alone, in front of a mirror near the bar. As they took a video of themselves being ridiculous, a sexy guy walked by and tried to get in on the action.

His name was Matteo. (Not really. But it was a name like Matteo.)

Needless to say, Jasmine fell for his cuteness, and he ended up leaving with the girls to hit up the local eatery (and by that, we mean McDonald's) for poutine.

As the three of them waltzed down the street with their artery-clogging food, they skipped hand-in-hand. At one point the topic of Matteo's penis came up (no idea why, but it happened), which led to the girls drunkenly touching the crotch of his pants as they stumbled down the street. (Yes, his pants were on. What kind of book do you think this is???)

When the evening came to an end, the three amigos headed to Jasmine's house. Matteo promptly flopped onto the couch and Jasmine went to the bathroom to prepare herself for a night of passion and rapture.

Nikki decided it would be hilarious to play a joke on Jasmine, so she laid down beside Matteo on the couch and told him to do something funny when Jasmine came back. Well, Matteo could barely function, let alone speak, at this point. He leaned over, grabbed Nikki's boob, and kissed her. Not the kind of joke she had in mind—but when Jasmine came out of the bathroom she only saw his hand resting on Nikki's boob and thought it was hilarious. I mean, this guy was just a random, anyway!

Nikki decided she'd leave the lovebirds alone and climbed into bed in the other room. Jasmine was ready to make the move on Matteo. That's when she encountered a problem she had not dealt with before—he was so drunk that, after a few failed attempts to arouse him, she had to accept there would be no action at all that night. She threw in the towel and climbed into bed with Nikki, leaving him to snore the night away alone.

The next morning, the girls awoke to the pitter-patter of man feet on their way to the bathroom. The next thing they knew, Matteo had flopped down in between them, laughing and cheerful as ever—despite obviously battling a horrific hangover. So there they stayed, all three of them, singing songs, sharing ridiculous stories, and just having a grand time. It was great, and Nikki even went to grab coffees for everyone. (Leaving Jasmine and Matteo to finally do the deed.)

They made breakfast together and spent the morning relaxing. Nikki was starting to think that this guy could be more than just a random for Jasmine. When she left in the early afternoon, Matteo was lying in bed with Jasmine, so she went into the room to say goodbye and leaned down for a hug.

That's when it hit her ... the smell of shit. She almost yelled out at how foul it was, but she literally couldn't speak because she couldn't breathe. It smelled like someone very sick had pooped their pants! Matteo had apparently farted and unleashed the worst smell either of the girls had ever encountered. They maintained composure, but Nikki wanted to burst out laughing, and Jasmine admitted later that she was completely repulsed. Someone you just had sex with should NOT smell like that!

Jasmine thought that maybe he had a bowel disorder or an allergy to something in their breakfast, so she decided to give him another chance.

A few days later, they hung out again. He showed her some of his kickboxing moves and then wrestled her onto the bed. That's when it happened again. The stench was back. Jasmine tried to avoid the awkwardness by ignoring the smell.

She might have overcome her gas-bomb revulsion, but when she went to use the bathroom (and take a deep breath), she found that Matteo had also peed on the toilet seat AND the floor! There was pee on the floor! Ugh, she was so grossed out!

It was a deal-breaker. Jasmine might have been able to get by the noxious clouds that Matteo emitted, but she knew deep down that she needed the type of man who can hit a target the size of a toilet bowl.

LESSONS LEARNED

1. McDonald's after a night out of drinking is basically a necessity, but a decision you will almost always regret.

2. Any guy over the age of 10 that still can't hit the toilet bowl when he's peeing needs some remedial training from his dad, not a girl-friend. (Guys: leaving your pee splashes for others to clean up is a disgusting habit that will prevent you from getting laid.)

3. Everybody farts. However, if a guy's farts are so deadly you can't breathe, you may have to let the poor bastard go. Breath is life.

THE TMI GUY

Candice told us a story about the last guy she dated, Cam, and we had to include it in the book because it has to do with poop, and we find that stuff ridiculously funny! It was a very new relationship and their first two weeks together were amazing. They had lots of laughs, excellent chemistry and terrific conversations. He was very thoughtful and caring; he'd message all day long, even if just to tell her he was thinking about her.

But. After week three, things changed. Cam became moody and very self-conscious. If he had a zit, he didn't want to go out, or he'd demand she use her makeup to cover it. His communication skills seemed to disappear, and suddenly there were days when Candice didn't hear from him until late in the evening or the next day.

It was around that time that one of Candice's friends invited them to her place for games night with a few other couples that Candice had known for a while. They decided to play a card game, and on the instructions, it said that the person who pooped most recently could go first.

Now, normally, since Candice had no shame, she'd be the person who would announce the exact moment that she had last had a bowel movement, and she'd probably add in details about consistency and amount. (We love this chick!) But since she was trying to impress her new beau, she kept a lid on it.

As everyone in the group awkwardly stated when their last poop was, Cam got up and excused himself to the bathroom, which was just off the living-room where they were all sitting.

Five minutes later he emerged to proudly announce that he "just took a shit" and would be going first.

Candice wanted to crawl under the ottoman to die, but she was too chubby to fit. She just sat there mortified. Here was a guy who had never met her friends, and now they were thinking about his bathroom routines. Thankfully, her friends laughed and, of course, Cam went first.

On their way back to Candice's place after, the weird, self-conscious behaviour re-emerged. He said he felt out of place because her friends' boyfriends and husbands were all better looking than him, and he was angry because he had a zit. She couldn't even see a zit! But his lack of confidence was so unappealing to her, especially combined with the image of him, well, strategically using the bathroom while her friends sat in the living room on the other side of the wall. (No one should want to win a game that badly!)

That night, as he tapped his erect penis against her leg, she realized she no longer found him attractive or sexy.

Candice decided she couldn't be with someone who had more self-esteem issues than she did. She gently but promptly dumped him the next day.

LESSONS LEARNED

1. New boyfriends should not announce that they've just taken a poopy ... ever, but especially in front of your friends.

2. No one should ever have to cover up someone else's zits unless they're a professional make-up artist.

I LOVE SALMON, BUT ...

> *One afternoon when we were at our close friend Patty's house for tea, she told us about a brutal dating experience she'd had. We were all ears. (You know how we love the dating war stories—we're writing a freakin' book about it!)*

At the time this story begins, Patty had just ended a long-term relationship she'd been in since high school and was looking to get back into the dating game. Right out of the gate, she met James, an attractive, athletic guy with a smile to die for and hair so incredible it looked like each strand was strategically placed on his head.

On his dating profile, James stated numerous times that he loved sushi and everything about sushi. Even his username had the word sushi in it. (WARNING!!) Patty found out later that he ate it daily— quelle surprise!

They met for dinner, and she was instantly attracted to him. They ended up back at his place, and let's just say it had been a while since Patty had had anything resembling good sex. Or sex at all. So it was on! Or was it?

They ended up on an air mattress, and those of you who've tried having sex on one will know how awkward it was. And partway through, when James was on top, Patty noticed a fishy smell coming from somewhere. It took just a few seconds for her to realize just how much he lived up to his username—it was like salmon was oozing from his pores.

Right after this realization hit her, she felt something wet dripping onto her face ... fishy smelling water ... no, not water, it was his sweat! The guy had seriously eaten so much fish that it was seeping from his body. The fuck. It was full-on dripping off him onto her face!!! She kept turning her head from side to side to try to avoid the drops and keep them from going into her mouth.

But when one salty, fishy drop landed straight in her eye, she was done. Patty never went back for sushi seconds!

LESSONS LEARNED

1. A man can only eat so much fish without becoming fishlike.

2. If a guy uses an air mattress as a bed, choose something with a more supportive surface! You could potentially leave with some major injuries.

I CAN'T STOP THINKING ABOUT YOUR UNDERWEAR

Jen went on a few dates with Ryan a number of years ago. He was a super nice guy, but she wasn't exactly feeling the sexual attraction she'd been hoping for.

She liked to give everyone a chance, and sometimes those things grow in time. (Hopefully, it doesn't take too long, 'cause a girl needs to get laid). On the third or fourth date, he invited her to his place for dinner.

She was hesitant because she figured he'd expect some kind of sexual encounter, and she still wasn't feeling it. But she decided to go so she could spend more time with him to see if maybe she'd develop more feelings. (And to get a free dinner.) He had a beautiful suite overlooking the ocean, so she hoped that a nice home-cooked meal, plus the view, would help stoke the fires of love.

He made a taco pie, something she'd never heard of. It tasted fine, and she appreciated the effort he put into making it—a lot of guys can't pull something like that off.

After dinner, they were on the couch watching a movie when Ryan slid over and they started making out. It was okay, nothing that blew her mind, but it obviously blew his. She could feel him rubbing his erection up against her leg, and he started grinding harder and harder until he made a weird face, moaned, and said, "Oh, my God—I just came in my pants."

This had never happened to Jen before. What was she supposed to say? Go and change your pants? She assumed that this is exactly what he'd do, but he didn't. He just sat there, in his soggy undies and stained jeans, while they finished the movie.

For Jen, the evening confirmed she just didn't have that loving feeling. Though he had some great qualities, Ryan just didn't do it for her.

She wasn't sure whether she should be happy that he'd had a wee bit of sexual pleasure despite her lack of electricity—or if she should have offered to spring for a pair of new underwear as a parting gift.

LESSONS LEARNED

1. A lot of us experimented with dry humping back in our younger years, and apparently, nothing has changed in some circles. A guy may still ejaculate in his underwear, and it's equally awkward when they're in their 30s. The good news is that their parents aren't in the next room like back in the day!

2. Taco and pie should be two separate food items. Never one.

RANDOM OCCURRENCES

CREEPY KITTY

A few months ago, Gayle was occasionally hooking up with a guy; let's call him Brian. Brian had a cat, Misty, that he described as a sweet little tortoiseshell gal with huge paws and a bubbly personality.

The first time Brian and Gayle hooked up, she decided she'd seduce him by coming out of the bathroom naked while he was watching TV. When she opened the bathroom door, though, she was greeted by Misty, sitting very still in the doorway and glaring up at Gayle in all her nakedness. Their eyes met, and Gayle felt like Misty was staring deep into her soul, judging her for tempting her human companion with a naked body in its full glory.

Gayle tried to step around the feline obstacle, since Misty wouldn't move—she just locked her eyes onto Gayle's private parts. Noticing the exchange, Brian laughed and said, "I guess she's a lesbian."

They had a chuckle and then got down to some slippery, slightly uncoordinated shower sex.

Afterward, Brian went to his bedroom to dress and Gayle stayed in the bathroom to dry off and fix her horrific soaking mop of hair.

She then went into the living room and sat on the couch waiting for Brian, and Misty jumped up beside her. Under different circumstances, this would be sweet—but there was no purring, just wide eyes with dark, dilated pupils. It was like Misty was questioning Gayle's very being.

Brian and Gayle cuddled up on the couch and were soon heading toward a second shag. As they got down to business, Gayle felt as if eyes were boring their way into the side of her head, and when she turned to look, there she was, the devil cat Misty, watching her every move. Brian laughed and swatted Misty off the couch, but Gayle was definitely feeling stage fright.

A moment later, Misty was on the couch again, two feet away from Gayle's face. They decided to finish off in the bedroom, and Brian closed the door so Misty couldn't partake in the action. Mid-session, Gayle heard desperate scratching and meowing at the door. Not just a sweet little meow; it was a deep howl. Gayle tried to block out the noise and focus, but it was so distracting—there was no way she could function at the sex intensity level she was used to.

That's when it happened: out of nowhere, Misty was up on the bed. How the hell had she gotten in?!

Later, Gayle would find out she'd gone through the bathroom and snuck into the bedroom through the en suite door, but at the time, it felt like some kind of powerful creepy-cat voodoo.

Gayle had had enough. Either the cat thought Gayle was a whore and was trying to protect Brian or she was totally jealous of Gayle's sexual moves. (Gayle liked to believe it was the latter.)

Gayle realized that, in addition to having a possessive (or possessed) cat, Brian didn't have the qualities she was looking for. She ended things—and Misty got her way.

LESSONS LEARNED

1. Never show up for a booty call without a supply of cat treats.

COFFEE SHOP STRUM-ALONG

A friend of ours was set up on a blind date a few years ago and agreed to let us tell her story.

They met at a local coffee shop after texting back and forth for a few days, and Sally was really looking forward to meeting Jerry in person.

The coffee shop was busy that day, but they managed to find a table near the back.

She was intrigued: he was cute, had a beautiful smile and seemed really friendly. He was carrying a guitar case, and as he hadn't mentioned he played the guitar, she asked him about it. He was more than willing to talk about his love for music. In fact, he pulled out his guitar and began strumming a tune.

Sally is pretty outgoing, but she felt the blood rush to her face and her heart rate increase as people looked their way curiously. She figured Jerry would just strum a little ditty and then put the guitar away after he'd demonstrated his skills, but no, he broke out into a full performance for all to hear, and everyone in the coffee shop turned to watch.

For Sally, it was one of those awkward "What do I do here?" moments. Should she start dancing? Clapping? Singing along? Ducking and running? She just let it ride out, head down, sipping casually on her coffee. The date ended rather quickly after that. She complimented him on his guitar skills (he was really talented!) and headed home.

They kept in touch, but never ended up having a second date, so Jerry may be strumming a tune in a coffee shop near you.

LESSONS LEARNED

1. If a guy brings a musical instrument on a first date, you have two choices:

    a. Hope he leaves it in the case (he could have a lesson after the date); or
    b. Pretend to be his manager.

$RICHIE RICH$

A few years back, not long after breaking up with her long-term boyfriend, Kennedy took to the city streets to find some new men. At a local pub, she met Ricky. He was nice, but not physically her type. He did, however, disclose that he was a millionaire—not exactly classy, but, hey, she wasn't really into him anyway. He gave her his number and asked if he could take her for dinner one night. She figured there was no harm in this, so she agreed.

But the night their dinner date was planned, Kennedy had such bad anxiety about meeting him she called to cancel. She couldn't put her finger on the reason why, but she just wasn't feeling it. He was very appreciative of the call since he said most girls just ghost him, so she felt like a decent human being!

A few months later he messaged to ask her out again. Once again, she committed; once again she cancelled. She knew she was making herself look like a total flake, but she had promised herself that she wouldn't date guys she wasn't interested in.

Another few months went by, and summer rolled around. Kennedy received a message from Ricky one evening with an invitation to bring some friends and go out on his yacht! She agreed to come by with a friend, thinking it would calm her nerves a bit and ensure the evening didn't read as a date. When the girls arrived at his place, they were blown away by how Jersey Shore it was. It was obviously a multimillion-dollar home, and he was wearing clothes that looked straight out of a Dolce & Gabbana store.

The evening on the yacht was great, turning into a party with lots of people. After they docked, everyone made their way back to Ricky's house and proceeded to drink way too much. Kennedy ended up getting obliterated and finally said, "I have to go home."

"Just stay here if you want," he replied suavely.

She mentally reviewed her plans for the next morning and, given that she had a 10 a.m. hair appointment just down the street, it made sense to sleep there and save some time in the morning. Instead of taking her to one of the other three bedrooms, he guided her to his room. But at that point, she was so drunk and tired she would have slept anywhere.

She flopped down on the bed, and he lay down beside her. He managed to sneak a kiss but she pulled away and turned over. He may have had a yacht and a pimpin' pad, but that didn't change the way she felt about him. She slept fully clothed, on top of the covers.

It was as hot as hell in the room, and she remembers wondering why a guy with all his money wouldn't spring for air conditioning. When she woke a few hours later, she turned over and found he was beside her, on his back on top of the covers, completely naked. All out for her to see! No shame in the dick game.

A moment later he stirred and got up to pee. Kennedy pretended to be asleep. She hoped he'd come back and say something like, "Oh, shit! I was so drunk I took my boxers off last night," but he lay back down, full frontal, and fell asleep.

His dick was definitely not the first thing she wanted to see in the morning. She wanted to see a cup of tea, a nice view, or a breakfast sandwich. She quietly got up out of bed, crept out of the room, shut the door and got the hell out of Dodge.

LESSONS LEARNED

——

1. If you feel you must cancel a date, there's a reason why—trust your gut!

2. If you cancel two dates you either have commitment issues OR your gut is screaming at you. Listen!

NEED SOME WATER WITH THAT FOOT?

Have you ever had a moment on a date when you would have traded your next vacation for a chance to turn back time an hour or two so you could start again from the top? Tracy has.

She met Ben online, and after chatting for a couple of days, they met up at one of the most ghetto coffee shops in the city. The plan was to meet there and then go for a walk along the waterfront. It was a beautiful day, and Tracy was kind of excited. Ben was younger than her by about eight years, but he seemed to have a great personality and was a lot of fun to talk to. That said, she tended to go for guys that have their careers set, or at least in motion. He was working three jobs just to make ends meet and hated them all. She figured a coffee and a walk couldn't hurt, though, so off she went!

She got to the coffee shop and had to pee in the worst way. The bathroom looked like a place where folk injected themselves with who knows what, or peed on the floor, or had sex, or—blah, we don't even want to think about it. The barista had to buzz her in, and there was a big sign outside saying the police would be called if there were any signs of drug use. She hovered above the toilet and used paper towel to turn the door handle.

She texted Ben to tell him where she was, in case he showed up and couldn't find her. Tracy figured she'd make a funny, you know, to break the ice—so she told him that it was the sketchiest bathroom and that she had to awkwardly hover above the toilet so as not to touch anything. She joked that she could have pee on her shoes and a side of herpes when he met her.

He responded with an "LOL," and when they met, he even checked her shoes for pee!!! What a guy, haha! They grabbed a coffee and went for a nice walk. She could tell he was really into her. He grabbed her hand partway through the date and even held her purse for her while she tied her shoes … ah bless!

As they walked back to her car, he asked if he could take her for dinner later in the week, but because she wasn't completely feeling it, she said she'd check her schedule.

(Eek, we've tried that one before!)

As she hugged him goodbye, he looked at her and said, "I do have to tell you something." Ah, here we go, she thought. What was it this time? She'd heard it all before. Or had she?

He said, "Remember earlier when you told me you might come out of the bathroom with a side of herpes? Well, I have herpes."

Tracy almost died right then and there. I mean, what are the chances?!? She felt terrible and apologized profusely. He laughed and said it wasn't a big deal; he just wanted to be honest.

(Which we completely admire!)

He told her he takes medication to keep it under control, and that it's nothing to worry about. Now she wouldn't consider this a deal breaker had she been really into him, but since she wasn't, it was just kind of the proverbial nail in the coffin. Still, after she left him, she did some research so that she could understand more about herpes and make an informed decision. She didn't want to be ignorant or rude without knowing more and even checked in with a doctor friend to get his view.

She ended up being straight with Ben that he just wasn't her type and apologized again for making a joke about herpes. He got a little bit defensive and told her she should do some research prior to making a judgment. She told him she had done that and had decided to be completely honest: she just didn't feel any chemistry, was looking for someone who had their life more on track and felt they were just too far apart in age.

Who would have thought that a joke about a dirty bathroom would lead to a story like this??? Damn.

LESSONS LEARNED

1. The only lesson learned here is to not make jokes about diseases. Ever. Again.

THE DISAPPEARING ACT

When Megan's friend Tanya started college, she immediately connected with a guy named Jack. They had a ton in common and loved spending time together. It was so nice to have his company during the long days of classes and studying.

Things went really well for a couple of months, and then they decided to have sex. After that, things seemed to fall apart. They continued to see each other, though, and one evening they went to a party together. There were lots of people mixing and mingling, and Tanya and Jack separated to chat with their friends. A few moments later Tanya saw Jack talking to another girl from their class. She didn't think anything of it until she saw him grab her hand and start to guide her upstairs. Well, we all know what happens at these house parties when couples go upstairs—it ain't board games. Tanya walked over to him and said, "What are you doing?" Jack stopped on the stairs, looked her in the eye, and just said, "Sorry."

Tanya was devastated, confused and embarrassed. The worst thing was that she had to see them all the time in class! It was painful. She kind of got over it, but just when she thought she had lost all feelings for Jack, he showed up and wanted to see her, so she caved. They started hooking up again. One evening he came over for a booty call, and when he arrived, she was in the shower. She yelled out to him that she'd be right there.

When she came out of the bathroom, he was gone. There was only a note that said, "Sorry, something came up."

> *How very Sex and the City of him.*

Tanya was infuriated. How could he do this to her? Well, she learned her lesson this time, and that was the last of Jack!

LESSONS LEARNED

1. If a guy ditches you at a party for another girl, HE IS A LOSER! You're better than that, girl!

2. If a guy arrives at your house for a booty call when you're in the shower, he should either get in the shower with you OR have a glass of wine waiting for you when you come out of the bathroom.

THE TRIP DRIP

Mary met Don while travelling in Europe, and it was love at first sight.

A lot of us have had those oversea flings—we'd like to know how many go anywhere!

They had an amazing connection. The only problem was that they lived in different countries, thousands of miles apart. After the trip, Mary went down to visit him a couple of times, and they always had an incredible time together. She felt she could see a future with him.

They'd long-distance dated for about a year when a friend announced she was moving to Florida with her dad, and Mary jumped at the chance to go down there to help them settle in. When Don found out, he suggested she come a few days early to stay with him and even offered to help pay for the plane ticket.

When he picked her up at the airport, though, she sensed something was wrong. But she chose to ignore it—she was just so happy to see him!

They went out for dinner that evening, and that's when Don introduced Mary to his new girlfriend!

What the hell!? Mary was so shocked and confused—why had he flown her down there when he had a girlfriend? He told her he didn't think he had a chance with the new girl, but they ended up connecting after Mary had already booked her flight, so he didn't have the heart to tell her.

Mary was heartbroken and was now thousands of miles away from home with nowhere to go. She had to call her friend's dad to come and pick her up from the restaurant and then spent the rest of the night crying.

What a waste of a trip. What a waste of a dream.

LESSONS LEARNED

1. Long-distance relationships are tough; be prepared for challenges and trust issues. (But hey, further along in the book you'll see that distance doesn't always matter when it comes to love!)

THE MEDICAL CRISIS

Joe and Lisa decided to go for a coffee and a walk; a pretty safe date. They met at a park and she was grateful to find he was fun to talk to.

As they walked, though, they noticed an elderly man sitting on the ground, with half of his body in the bushes.

Lisa was alarmed—was he sleeping? Another woman ran over and started to pull the man onto the grass. Joe and Lisa went over and realized the man wasn't moving, so they called 911 and asked for an ambulance. Lisa ran up to the top of the hill by the road to wait for the ambulance (which left her huffing and puffing and her first-date hair ruined) while Joe waited with the man to make sure he was still breathing.

The ambulance arrived and took the poor fellow away.

The whole ordeal only took about an hour from start to finish, but it was tough to get back into the date groove afterwards.

Although she was impressed with his heroic nature, Lisa decided that Joe wasn't really her type.

LESSONS LEARNED

1.   Learn CPR. You could save a life!

WILD

> *We sat down with a friend of ours one evening, and when the topic of dating came up, she generously divulged one of her most uncomfortable experiences.*

Katie met Mitchell online, and though he lived over an hour away, he wanted to meet her so badly he drove to her hometown just for dinner.

As Katie pulled up to meet him, she was pleasantly surprised to see that he was actually BETTER looking than his photos.

> *We've all been duped on this one before, so things were already looking up!*

As they chatted on their way to the restaurant, Mitchell stopped outside a novelty store. The store was closed, but he peered in the window, going on and on about the random shit it sold: zapping mosquito rackets, bizarre signs, wigs—you name it, they probably had it.

Katie was hungry and a little weirded out, but she smiled and nodded.

They finally got to the restaurant and took their seats. When the waitress came over to introduce herself, Mitchell cut her off, stood up, and formally introduced himself. Sweet—but super-awkward for all.

Mitchell told Katie that he had lived on the coast but was in terrible debt and so had decided to move to a smaller city and live in a tent. Yes, a tent. He not only lived in a tent, he lived in a tent in the woods, behind the local university.

Katie is a girlie-girl, so she, of course, wanted to know how he cleaned himself. He told her that he had gone to the "higher ups" in the university nearby and they'd agreed to let him shower and use the bathroom there.

Things couldn't possibly get further outside of Katie's comfort zone, right? Oh no, they did. He pulled out his phone and told her he wanted to show her a picture of his best friend. It was a squirrel. It was a photo of Mitchell with a piece of granola in his hand and his friend the squirrel casually munching down on the treat. He went on to explain how sweet the squirrel was and how often they spent time together.

Not soon enough for Katie, the bill came. When the waitress asked if they'd pay together or separately, Mitchell informed them both that it would be separate, and then stated he doesn't pay on the first date "because it's expected." Katie bit her lip and even offered to pay for his dinner, but he declined. He walked her to her car and attempted to move in for a kiss but she dodged.

The next day, he texted her to say he'd had a great time and said he understood if his living situation was an issue for her.

Katie told him that she didn't think they would be a good match. He went on his way, and she realized there was no way she'd ever be able to spend the night with a guy who didn't even own a mattress, let alone have running water.

LESSONS LEARNED

1. Perhaps ask about a guy's living situation before you meet. Unless you're the kind of woman who thinks wild men who live in the woods are super-hot, you probably won't get past overnighting without a bathroom or phone charger.

2. If a guy has to publicly announce that he's not paying for the bill, we suggest losing him. We get that some people prefer to split the bill on dates. Fair enough. What we don't get is when a guy has to make a pronouncement about it. Not cool! Just say, "Shall we split this?" and it's all good, bro.

THE DRIVER

I know it might seem like we sit around with our friends and talk about guys while drinking wine all the time—but that's not all we do. We eat as well.

One evening recently, on a girls' wine night, our friend Becca told us the story of her worst date ever.

It took place when she was 18 and she's now in her 30s, yet she remembers it like it was yesterday!

Becca worked in a late-night café, and a few evenings a week, a good-looking guy would come in, always dressed in a nice suit. They chatted at his table for about a month and then he worked up the courage to ask her out.

They decided to go for a walk one evening after she got off work. Ian had an amazingly chiselled body, and Becca asked him why he always dressed so nicely. She guessed that he might be a waiter, doorman or perhaps some kind of private security person. He told her he was "in the industry." When she looked at him blankly, unclear on what industry he was referring to, he explained sheepishly that he was a stripper.

At 18, Becca was kind of fascinated by the idea, so she asked him all about it. He loved her attention, so much so that he undid his pants, revealed his sparkly G-string and performed a few of his moves.

After they'd walked for a while, Becca noticed that he was sweating a lot and the conversation started getting weird. He seemed disoriented and talked about six degrees of separation, the universe and rather random facts. He then looked at Becca with a glazed expression on his face, as if he didn't recognize her. At one point, he reached out to touch her face in an odd way.

They got back to the car, climbed in, and drove off. It was then that he started speeding, running red lights, missing turns and basically scaring the shit out of Becca.

What was happening?! He raced down the street, heading towards a cliff. It was then that Becca snapped into survival mode, reached over and turned the wheel. That seemed to snap him back to reality, and he slowed down and pulled into a gas station. He started ranting about wanting to see if she was real or just a figment of his imagination.

Becca was crying and ran into the gas station. He followed her inside, grabbed five chocolate bars, ate every single one and dropped the wrappers on the floor. (Becca watched all of this while hiding behind a rack of chips.)

A few moments later he seemed to be completely normal again. He apologized profusely and finally told her that he had diabetes and hadn't eaten for hours.

It was the weirdest, most terrifying experience of her life, one that she wouldn't do over! He did ask if he could call her, but Becca voted no. She wisely figured that fearing for your life on the first date was basically a sign you shouldn't go for a second.

LESSONS LEARNED

1. Getting in a car with a stranger is dangerous. Do not do it, no matter how sparkly his thong is, unless you have a full medical report in hand.

THE ZERO-NIGHT STAND

Many years ago, Candace met a bartender who worked at a restaurant she frequented downtown. After noticing him, she frequented it even more. She thought Liam was gorgeous and was thrilled when she managed to find out that he felt the same about her.

They chatted at the restaurant on a regular basis, and her friends pushed her to go out with him. Finally (finally!) he asked her out, and she was stoked.

They planned to meet for drinks, and she went all out—dressed to the nines; hair and makeup on point. She texted him to confirm their meeting time, but he didn't respond. She continued to text him, as she was concerned, but she never heard anything back.

There she was, a smoke show with nowhere to go.

The next day, he messaged her, apologizing profusely. He said he was so sorry and wanted to try again. He had a million and one excuses as to why he bailed, and because Candace (bless her heart) believed in second chances, she agreed to a second date.

This time it was drinks and a walk on the beach at lunchtime, since he had to work that night—and it actually happened. They had a great time, and she really enjoyed his company; the fact that he was super cute was just a bonus.

They planned another date (second? third?) for dinner. Annnnnd ... he stood her up again. This time she was so pissed she rounded up a group of her friends for backup and confronted him at work.

He saw her walk in and quickly ran over. He was very embarrassed and talked a mile a minute. Her girlfriends ruthlessly taunted him to provide a good excuse as to why he would ditch their friend.

All he could say was, "I feel bad—please, please, please let me make it up to you." But Candace (wisely) felt their ship had sailed.

She continued to frequent the restaurant, though, and he never backed down on asking her out. He bought her drinks every time she went in (which was a good reason to keep going).

A few weeks later, her best friend Grant came into town, and they decided to go out to eat. Since the restaurant where Liam worked was one of the only decent places to eat nearby, Candace decided to take Grant there. During dinner, he noticed Liam staring at Candace and smiling. When he sent drinks over to their table, Grant asked, "What's with that guy? Something going on with you two?"

Candace told him about the multiple times he had stood her up.

Grant listened intently and then said, "Hey—you've always said you want to have a one-night stand before you meet 'the one.' He should be it!"

Liam did seem like a perfect one-night-stand kinda guy. Candace definitely wouldn't get attached as she already knew he was kind of an unreliable dick, so she wouldn't care if she never heard from him again. Completely ignorant of the relevant rules, she continued drinking until she had the nerve and then approached Liam at the bar and blurted, "We should have sex!"

After he agreed (big shock) she awkwardly said, "Tonight doesn't work for me, but how about Saturday?"

> *This may be the most planned-in-advance one-night stand in the history of one-night stands!*

Saturday night rolled around, and again Candace and Grant went for dinner, but to a different location. After, she dropped him off at the place he was staying and went home to prep for her first ever one-night stand.

She soon heard a knock on the door, and there was Liam, gorgeous as ever. But he was noticeably inebriated—and he'd brought his dog.

Her first thought was, "It's probably a good thing—I'm a little tipsy too." And while her building was strictly no pets, who would know?

They started making out, which led to stumbling into the bedroom. She pulled out her usual tricks to get the old penis standing at attention but, no matter what she did, it remained flaccid.

Finally, she blurted out, "Um, sooooo, are you going to get hard?"

He apologized, blaming it on the booze. They continued to fool around, but to no avail. He just couldn't get a hard-on. Finally, she got up and excused herself, heading to the bathroom to calm herself down and give him a moment to deal with whatever his issue was.

When she came back into the bedroom, she found him cocooned in her blanket, lying with his feet on her pillow (ewww) and his head at the bottom of the bed. What the hell!? She grabbed the blanket and pulled with all her might. "What are you doing?" she said.

"I'm sorry, I'm sorry!" he said, and then he grabbed her and pulled her onto the bed to start making out with her again. Yet again, he couldn't get a boner.

Since she'd never had a one-night stand, Candace was at a loss as to what to do here. Instead of kicking him out, which is what some (most) of us would do, she casually suggested they just go to sleep.

An hour later, he started thrashing around in bed and moaning. He rolled over towards the window and grabbed onto the ledge before reaching up and ripping her curtains, rod and all, right off the wall.

There were just giant holes where the rod had been attached.

The dog, which Candace had almost forgotten about by now, started barking frantically, ensuring the neighbours would all be awake too. So now she was yelling at the dog to be quiet, he was barking, and Liam was standing there with a curtain rod in hand, once again apologizing profusely.

"I'm so sorry," he said. "I've liked you for so long. I think you're beautiful and I'm totally messing this up!"

"Yes, yes, you are! You stood me up twice! You shouldn't even BE here right now, and then you show up drunk and wreck my place?!"

He stood staring at her for a moment. She could see the wheels in his mind turning and wondered what version of apology he'd come up with next. But she was completely unprepared, even so.

"I'm so sorry," he said, yet again. "You're SO much hotter than my girlfriend."

"YOUR GIRLFRIEND??"

Candace lost it and yelled at him to get out of her apartment. He had the nerve to ask to use the bathroom before leaving, and while she sat in the living room fuming, she had to listen to him vomiting into the toilet. He finally left, and she slammed the door behind him.

Five minutes later, he came back for his dog leash.

Thankfully, Candace is now settled down and looks back on her adventures with Liam as a laugh—and yet another reason to be grateful for the amazing guy she met soon after.

LESSONS LEARNED

1. Okay, this is an old chestnut, we know, but it bears repeating until we all remember it no matter how hot he is: "Stand me up once, shame on you. Stand me up twice, shame on me."

2. If you think you can separate your feelings from sex, then, by all means, have a (safe!) one-night stand! It's either going to be a memorable night or material for our next book.

3. Over-drinking can lead to limp dicks, wall damage, barking dogs, and the smell of vomit in your bathroom. If he shows up drunk, call him a cab, STAT. Nothing is worth that potential clean-up.

THE CHEESE MONITOR

A few months after Deb's divorce, she decided it was time to get back into the dating scene, so she joined an online site. Right off the bat, she matched with Derek. He was good looking and had an amazing bod—he obviously worked out a lot. She was pleasantly surprised when he messaged her and asked her to meet for dinner and drinks.

It would be Deb's first date in years, and she wasn't really sure what to expect, but she put on her big-girl panties and off she went.

They met at a pub and found a quiet table. She was attracted to him physically, especially his body. They decided to share a charcuterie board (who doesn't like a good meat 'n' cheese platter?) and ordered some wine. After a few minutes of casual conversation and nibbling, Derek said, "I hope you don't always eat that much cheese."

Deb recoiled from the cheese board. Did he really just make a comment about how much she was eating???

He followed up that gem of social intelligence with, "How often do you work out? 'Cause I can only date a girl that works out on a regular basis."

She almost choked on the cheese she was no longer enjoying, questioning her life choices in general. She told him she went to the gym a couple of times a week, to which he replied, "That's not really enough."

The conversation that followed was awkward, and Deb felt really uneasy. She'd agreed to go to a movie with him after dinner, though, so they sat through a film. She sipped from her bottle of water while he ate his popcorn with great relish. When the credits rolled, he tossed his uneaten popcorn down toward the first row, adding embarrassment to Deb's general mortification.

We're guessing Derek is still single, probably lifting weights in front of a mirror at the gym.

LESSONS LEARNED

1. If a guy comments on how much you're eating on a date, put down your fork, go to the bathroom and then head out the back door. Perhaps after stealing some food off of his plate, just to rub it in.

2. If a guy comments on how often you should go to the gym, put down your fork, go to the bathroom and then head out the back door. Or just leave through the front door. Don't say goodbye— really, no further conversation is necessary. He'll eventually figure it out, and you will be doing a valuable service to the entire female population.

3. If a guy over the age of five throws popcorn anywhere other than in the garbage at the movie theatre—use the front entrance or the back, either way. (Not a euphemism, in this case.)

THE SHORTEST STORY IN THE BOOK

Lisa was excited to meet James. They'd been chatting online for about a week, and he seemed like a genuinely normal guy. They agreed he'd pick her up and they'd go to the local pub.

When he arrived, she opened the door to get into his car, and there he sat, completely naked.

Without saying anything at all, Lisa calmly closed the door and walked back into her house.

The end.

LESSONS LEARNED

1. Be like Lisa. If your date shows up naked (or with his penis in his hand) (yes, that happened) (more than once), get the hell out of there.

HAPPY ENDINGS
(No, not those ones.)

F*CK THE PLAN

Carrie has had her fair share of bad relationships, including one with a man who ended up in jail for assaulting her.

She was at a point in her life where—at some deep level—she felt maybe she didn't deserve an amazing guy, like she wasn't worth it and she'd never find love.

She decided to take a couple of months to do some self-reflection and writing. She wrote down what she was looking for in a man and the things about herself that she wanted to work on so that she was ready to love and to be loved. She read a lot of self-help books, spent time with family and friends, and forgot about men for a time.

When she finally decided to start dating again, she had a plan. She was going to find the love of her life, and that was that! She joined an online dating site and went on two to three dates a day—yes, PER DAY. She was bound and determined to find the right man for her. She met a few good guys (and a few weird ones), but they just didn't have what she was looking for.

She now knew what she wanted, and she wasn't afraid to weed through the frogs to find her prince. After eight days of daily dates, she got a message from Brian. She really liked his profile, they seemed to have a lot in common, and he was sexy to boot!

Now we have to add in here—during her time of self-reflection, Carrie had a tarot card reading. One of the cards told her that she'd find the love of her life soon, another said she'd get whatever she wanted over the next year, and one told her that told her there'd be a death in the family.

Back to our story ...

Carrie decided to meet Brian for breakfast one Sunday. Sadly, she woke to a call from her father telling her that her grandmother had passed away. Obviously, she was upset, and she texted Brian that she wouldn't be able to make their date because there'd been a death in her family. He urged her to at least come for coffee; he wanted to try to cheer her up and promised he'd do all the talking. She liked his persistence and decided that she'd rather meet him than sit at home upset. When she walked into the restaurant, she was greeted with his big grin and sweet face. There was an immediate physical attraction, and as promised, he did all the talking!

In fact, she barely got a word in edgewise and was even a bit concerned that he didn't seem to want to know anything about her. They said goodbye and Carrie headed home, unsure if this would go anywhere.

She was greeted by a text from Brian saying he'd had a great time, and even though he was sure she was getting a slew of messages from guys, he'd like a chance at another date. She agreed but continued to chat with and date other guys.

The following weekend she made plans with Brian but ended up cancelling to go out with another guy she was interested in and had been seeing a bit longer. In the past, when Carrie had cancelled plans with a guy, she'd either been insulted or ghosted, so she was prepared for the worst. She was pleasantly surprised to find Brian was okay with it and followed up by asking when she was free next. Deep down, she wondered if he was too good to be true. He had everything she was looking for, except a big family (something she'd always wanted, since she came from a broken home).

Still, she went on a date with the other guy, who took her to meet his family. (He was clearly smitten.) It went relatively well until he pulled up some videos that he found hilarious and she found ridiculously stupid. Sharing a similar sense of humour was one of the top 10 on her must-have list.

She then realized she'd been thinking about Brian and missing him. When the date ended, she texted him to find out when he was free again.

This time, he didn't respond nearly as quickly, and Carrie worried that she had ruined something that might have been great. The next day, at about 3 p.m., after a long night of partying (that she could have taken part in had she not cancelled), Brian messaged her back. They met up the following day, and then the next day, and the day after that. They spent the entire week together! After all avenues of the relationship were explored (bow chicka wow wow), Carrie knew he was the one.

Lying in bed together the next morning, Carrie looked at him and asked if he wanted to get married. It just felt so right. She'd never felt a love like this before, and in the way everything has worked out in their relationship so far, he felt the same way.

He said he had wanted to ask her but was afraid she would think he was crazy. Turns out, they were equally crazy!!! He said he'd marry her in a heartbeat and told her to go out and pick a ring, any ring she wanted. They were married a few months later and now have a beautiful baby boy.

So, even for those of us who feel hopeless and undeserving, love is waiting for us somewhere.

Maybe loving ourselves is the first step to finding the love we deserve.

LESSONS
LEARNED

■■■■■■

1. Find yourself before you try to find "the one." Sometimes we think we know ourselves, but deep down we're still searching for something to fill the gaps we feel in our lives. How can someone love us when we can't love ourselves?

2. Take your time. Date; enjoy meeting people. When your Prince Charming comes along, he'll steal your heart when you least expect it!

The End (As If!)

We know that most of our stories have sad endings, but we couldn't leave you feeling down and out.

As Carrie's story shows, happy endings do exist. The girl meets the man of her dreams, her prince, her knight in shining armour—sometimes it just takes a few bumps in the road to get there.

Despite our own share of bad dates, we believe in love and happiness ever after. There are good guys out there, and there is at least one waiting for you. (And a couple waiting for us!)

MEGAN: Although Janet and I have had epically horrible dates for years, the Und8ables really started with the TV show *First Dates Canada.*

On the morning of my episode, a bird did his business on my arm as I walked to my hair appointment. Random start to a story, I know, but you'll get my point in a minute. People always say that it means good luck when a bird poops on you. In that moment, I felt the experience I was about to have would be life-changing. I thought I would meet the love of my life that night—I didn't. But now, a year or so later, I know that it did change my life, in an even better way than I'd imagined.

I met Janet at the audition for the show. We had both cancelled our originally scheduled audition times and switched to the same time slot. Without that coincidence, it's likely we never would have crossed paths. Now we are close to completing our book. Who knows how far I'd be in the writing process without my partner in crime?

So, Ms. Und8able, I want you to be as happy as you can be as the fabulous, single girl that you are! When you least expect it, a bird will poo on you (or something like that) and it will be the start of a new adventure. And it will be amazing. xxx

---

JANET: I never really imagined I'd write a book, let alone do it with a friend that I met through random circumstances, but what a journey it's been! Megs, thank you for taking on this endeavour with me! I couldn't imagine doing it with anyone else—it's been a crazy ride and I'm so thankful to have been on it with you!

I admittedly have struggled with being single and truly LOVING it. (Some of you girls do, and I admire that!) As women, I think we should embrace the time we have alone, because if we can't love hanging out with ourselves, how will anyone else love being around us?!?

We have years and years of our lives to spend with "the one," and I'd rather discover myself first than end up changing 10 or 20 years in and driving someone completely nuts (or vice versa). When I fall in love with the right guy, I want to know he loves me for who I am, the good and the bad!

I also don't want to end up waking up beside someone who bores me. I want to laugh, learn, argue, make up and fall in love with him over and over again.

We all want to create our own "happy ending," and I wish you all the luck in the world on finding yours, whether it be with your beautiful, awesome self, or with the love of your life.

Thank you for reading!

MEGAN & JANET, PEACE OUT ...

Well, there's only so much drama we can fit into one little book. (Cough! Sequel! Cough!) When we met over a year ago, who knew we'd be finishing a book?!

(Megan: Well, I knew all along!)
(Janet: Eye roll.)

We hope, if you were feeling down about dating and single life, that this book made you laugh a bit (or a lot!). At the very least, you now know that:
    a. Girl, it's not you, it's them; and
    b. You're not alone out there, girlfriend—not even close.

Maybe we've given you a bit of hope in your dating life. Perhaps these stories helped you realize that there are many incredible single women out there going through dating purgatory as well! (Or maybe you're a woman at a crossroads in a relationship who wanted a laugh as well as a reminder that the single life ain't all it's cracked up to be.)

Whatever your story, whatever your journey, we're so glad you chose to take us along with you.

For the two of us, it's a new chapter in our lives and we can't wait to see where it takes us. (See what we did there? Book?! Chapter?!? Okay, moving on.)

Throughout the writing process, we have told our own stories and enjoyed a glass or two of wine with other incredible women who were willing to tell us their stories. There have been lots of laughs and gasps along the way, as well as tears and even the occasional argument! This was truly a labour of love and it's only just begun.

To all the hard-working, single, empowered females out there, we salute you!!!

Love,

The Und8ables, *Megan and Janet*
xxx

ACKNOWLEDGMENTS

The Und8ables want to thank all of the people who worked on and believed in this book as much as we did. We could barely apply eyeliner without screwing it up, and now we've written a book! Thank you to our family and friends, some of whom were shocked at the content at first but still supported our crazy dream of having it published. Lastly, we'd like to thank the amazing women who drank lots of wine with us and then courageously (yet willingly) shared the stories of their dating disasters—this book wouldn't have come to life without you! We'll have a wine night with all of you once we sell a million copies, but this time, it won't be the cheap shit.

93276529R00102

Made in the USA
Columbia, SC
07 April 2018